FOREWORD

The Chartered Institution of Water and Environmental Management (CIWEM) is a multi-disciplinary professional and examining organization for engineers, scientists and other professional personnel engaged in water and environmental management. It was formed in July 1987 by the unification of three eminent organizations, The Institution of Public Health Engineers, The Institution of Water Engineers and Scientists and the Institute of Water Pollution Control, each having a history of some 100 years.

Over the years the predecessor bodies have produced definitive manuals and other publications, notably in respect of British practice in the water industry. These have become reference sources for those who are actively engaged in the field, as well as for students seeking authoritative guidance in preparing for professional qualifications.Such publications are being continued by CIWEM, and the range is being extended to take account of the wider environmental issues and interests which the new organization now embraces.

This introductory booklet on *Wastes Management* is the first of a series to be published by CIWEM on an aspect of environmental management which is today giving rise to increasing concern, particularly in respect of the treatment and disposal of special and hazardous wastes. Although it is intended as an introduction to the subject, and has been written as a general guide to the interested layperson, the booklet provides a comprehensive summary of the situation in the UK, and should also be useful to those embarking on a career in the field.

The Institution wishes to record its thanks to those members who have contributed to the production of the booklet, and in particular to Mrs Jane Barron who has been responsible for the preparation of the text.

DR R.A. BAILEY
President

ACKNOWLEDGEMENTS

The Institution gratefully acknowledges permission from the following to reproduce plates:

Aspinwall & Company Ltd. (Plate 7)

W. S. Atkins (Plates 6 and 9)

Biffa Waste Services Ltd. (Plates 2, 5 and 8)

Cleanaway Ltd. (Plates 1 and 4)

The Waste Company (Plate 3)

CONTENTS

FIGURES

PLATES

TABLES

ABBREVIATIONS USED IN THE TEXT

COPA	Control of Pollution Act 1974
COTC	Certificate of Technical Competence
DAFS	Department of Agriculture and Fisheries for Scotland
DoE	Department of the Environment
EPA	Environmental Protection Act 1990
HMIP	Her Majesty's Inspectorate of Pollution
HWI	Hazardous Waste Inspectorate
ISO	International Standards Organization
LAWDC	Local Authority Waste Disposal Company
LWRA	London Waste Regulation Authority
MAFF	Ministry of Agriculture, Fisheries and Food
NFFO	Non-Fossil Fuel Obligation
Nirex	Nuclear Industry Radioactive Waste Executive
NRA	National Rivers Authority
PCB	Polychlorinated biphenyl
RDF	Refuse-derived fuel
RPA	River Purification Authority (Scotland)
WAMITAB	Waste Management Industries' Training and Advisory Board
WCA	Waste Collection Authority
WDA	Waste Disposal Authority
WRA	Waste Regulation Authority

1. THE NEED TO MANAGE WASTES

Waste is something for which we have no further use and which we wish to get rid of. It can be solid or liquid, and includes waste products arising from our way of life and waste body products. Wastes therefore range from the materials which are discarded in household dustbins (tin cans, bottles, vegetable trimmings) and flushed down our toilets (sullage, sewage) to the by-products of chemical processes (brewing, pharmaceuticals, electroplating), agricultural waste (straw, manure) and the wastes produced by the nuclear industry. Definitions and classifications of various wastes are given in the Glossary.

The early 1990s have seen a significant change in the way that we manage wastes in the UK. UK and EU legislation has reflected the public attitude of conservation, re-use and sustainable development. Public awareness generally has been heightened by the United Nations Conference on the Environment and Development in Rio, June 1992. The output of the Conference: Agenda 21, Chapter 21, specifically referred to the environmentally sound management of solid wastes. There is an international acknowledgement that wastes should not be simply dumped in the most convenient, cheapest manner by the waste producer, who may then walk away from the resulting environmental pollution.

In the UK, responsibility has been placed firmly on the producer of the waste to ensure that it is properly and safely managed — whether through recycling, treatment or disposal — minimizing the potential for damage to the environment or harm to human health. This concept is called the Duty of Care (see Chapter 3).

The technical and professional standing of practitioners in the waste industry has been radically altered by legislation, brought into force in 1994, requiring practitioners to hold a certificate of technical competence (COTC — see Chapter 3). This means that only technically competent persons will now be allowed to run waste management facilities. The COTC became a requirement under the new Wastes Management Regulations brought into force in 1994.

These Regulations have also attempted to prevent waste managers from dissociating themselves from environmental damage their actions have caused. The regulations considerably expand previous legislation, requiring all wastes management facilities to be licensed. Where activities to do with wastes management are exempt from licensing, they must still be registered with the local authority. Registration is also required of any carrier of waste (see Chapter 3) or any waste broker (and this includes consultants acting on behalf of their clients). Thus, all waste management activities should be known to the local authority.

Licences for wastes management facilities will only be granted to persons who can show: (a) that they have not been convicted of a relevant offence, and (b) that they have made adequate financial provision to remedy any environmental damage or harm to human health that may result from their facility. Licence holders can no longer hand in their licences at a time of their own choosing: they have to satisfy the regulation authority that the facility will not cause damage to the environment or harm to human health, now or in the future. In this way it is hoped to ensure that the polluter pays principle will be established and engender a more responsible attitude towards wastes management.

Waste is classified according to its source and according to the hazards associated with its handling and final disposal, i.e. danger to public health and the environment. Special classifications are given to wastes which present a particular hazard with respect to public health, i.e. hazardous, special and radioactive, and there are particular controls governing the management of these wastes. For the various categories of waste which are considered in this booklet, the total estimated arisings in the UK alone amount to about 505 million tonnes per year. By way of comparison, this is almost equal to the total world production of iron.

Figure 1 shows that, whilst the vast majority of UK wastes are of agricultural origin, large quantities originate from mining and quarrying activities. The disposal of these particular wastes is relatively free of legislative control and they are generally disposed of back to the land by the producer. Such wastes are not covered in any great detail in this booklet. The management of the remaining wastes shown in Figure 1 (148 million tonnes) is strictly controlled by legislation. Of these, industrial and demolition wastes comprise the greatest proportion, being approximately three and a half times the volume of wastes arising from domestic households.

Hazardous and special wastes scarcely seem significant in terms of tonnage; similarly radioactive waste arisings are low when compared to total waste arisings.

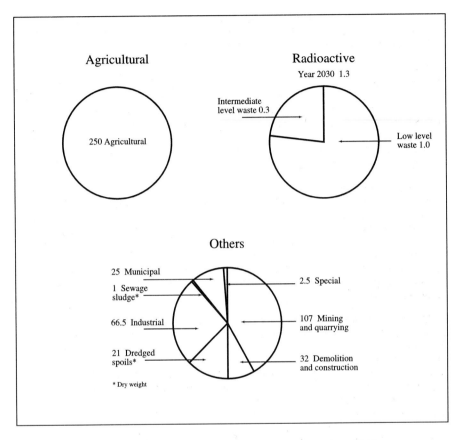

Fig. 1 Waste arisings (in million tonnes) during 1990
(*Digest of Environmental Protection and Water Statistics,* No 14, 1991
and *Waste Management Paper 1,* Second Edition 1992)

However, these relatively small tonnages of waste (hazardous, special and radioactive) actually require more expertise for their handling and treatment and more stringent controls on their ultimate disposal than do other wastes, making them the most costly to manage in terms of £/tonne.

The majority of wastes in the UK are disposed of to land, the sheer volume being useful for filling disused quarries and reclaiming marginal lands. However, the results of the 1993 Waste Monitoring Survey *Waste Disposal in the South East Region* suggest that all usable void in the region will be filled by 2004; sites with existing planning permission will have been filled by 1999.

For this and other reasons, the government is actively seeking ways to promote recycling and the use of incineration with energy recovery (see Chapter 5). Local authorities have been set a target of recycling 25 per cent of domestic wastes by the year 2000 and householders are encouraged to recycle constituents of their wastes. Bottle, can, paper and textile banks are a familiar sight in major supermarket car parks, council car parks and recycling centres. The public bring their waste to these locations and deposit it themselves in the banks. Less familiar are the segregated kerb collection systems run by some district councils. Householders are given a container with compartments for say, paper, glass, cans and plastics, and weekly collections are made. However, despite the strenuous efforts of both district councils and a fairly large proportion of householders, the proportion of wastes recycled is unlikely to rise much above the current average of 3.8 per cent of household waste, unless a commercial demand is generated for the recycled materials. There is currently little or no commercial incentive for manufacturers to use recycled materials in preference to virgin raw materials. However, public pressure has forced the use of recyclable materials for the packaging of supermarket goods; it is to be hoped that pressure for the use of other recycled materials will follow.

Public awareness of the dangers arising from the mismanagement of wastes has been aroused by a number of incidents, the most notable of which in the UK have been the discovery by children of cyanide waste in the Midlands (in the early 1970s) and the destruction of part of a bungalow in Derbyshire (in 1986) which was caused by an explosion arising from the presence of landfill gas. Many people also know of the story of Love Canal in the USA where a residential development was built over a hazardous waste dump. Chemical contamination and toxic gases came to the surface, poisoning the ground, and were thought to have given rise to miscarriages in pregnant women, and disease and medical defects in both children and adults, resulting finally in an evacuation of the area. Although such an extreme scenario may seem unlikely in the UK, there have been cases where residents have had to be moved from their homes when it has been discovered that these were built on or near to old hazardous waste disposal sites. One of the most well known is the Glory Hole in Portsmouth: an old disposal site where residential blocks had been built for and inhabited by Services personnel. Following considerable media attention, these people were relocated whilst a risk assessment of the real (rather than the perceived) hazard was carried out.

Certain other incidents related to the incineration of wastes have caught the media's attention and have become emotive issues. Whilst there can be no doubt that certain discharges from industrial plants (including those used for waste treatment) can contain harmful substances, emission limits are prescribed to protect the environment and human health. Diseases blamed on such facilities are known statistically to cluster at random and, whilst emotion may readily link postulated cause with observed effect, in practice it is much harder to establish a true cause/effect relationship on the basis of currently-recognized facts.

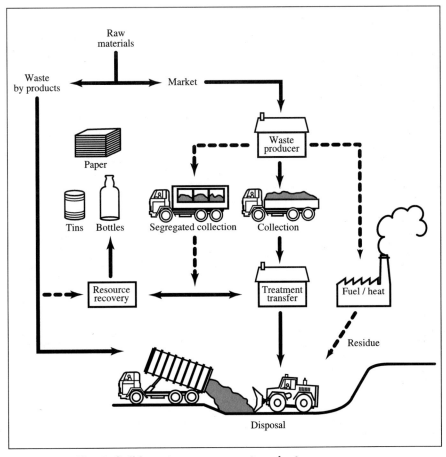

Fig. 2 Solid waste management: mainstream process

Some years ago (1988) it was reported that ships carrying, in one case, household waste and in another, hazardous waste, were cruising the world's oceans seeking acceptable disposal sites (on land) for their cargo. The UK had been seen by some as a suitable recipient country for USA-generated household waste, and various plans were put forward to landfill[1] these wastes here, generally linked to the production of landfill gas as a commercial by-product. Whilst at the time the government intervened to prevent this happening, it remains keen to capitalize on the UK's technical expertise and physical resources, and to promote the importation of hazardous waste for treatment at commercial sites. Some 44 000 tonnes of hazardous wastes were imported to England and Wales in 1990/91 for this purpose.

A public awareness of the emotive issues which are associated with waste management serves to reinforce the concept that the wastes management industry must be managed and controlled as rigorously as any other commercial industry. Figure 2 depicts the simplified process stream for the solid waste industry, from the incorporation of raw materials into a product to the final disposal of the used article. Each step of the process must be carefully controlled to maximize efficiency and to comply with legislation which is intended to protect both public health and the environment.

It should be noted that whilst waste management practices in England and Wales are similar, they are different in Scotland and Northern Ireland. This is due to the different legal and administrative systems in these countries, resulting in a different structure for waste disposal and regulation and also for water protection.

It was felt that it would be premature to anticipate the precise nature of proposed new legislation in this booklet. However, the Institution has a specialist panel, the Waste Management Panel, which is able to give advice on certain matters, specifically waste management[2].

---

[1] 'Landfill' is the term used for the controlled disposal of wastes to land.

[2] Readers who are interested in up-to-date information should contact the Institution's Headquarters.

2. LEGISLATIVE BACKGROUND

INTRODUCTION

The principal driving force in environmental legislation, including waste and wastes management, is the European Union. All recent UK domestic legislation, such as the Water Act 1989 and the Environmental Protection Act 1990, has been strongly influenced by the need to comply with and implement EC Directives.

Current UK legislation with regard to solid wastes exists to give planning and pollution control, as well as implementing EC Directives. Additional legislation exists to monitor the movement and final disposal of hazardous wastes. A brief history of the legislation relevant to solid waste management is given in the following section. Major current legislative provision is described in Chapter 3. It should be noted that for Scotland some of the legislation has different dates from those shown, and in some cases may not apply. In Northern Ireland, the legislation is again different.

LEGISLATIVE BACKGROUND

Public Health Act 1848 (superseded)

Although some local environmental legislation existed before this date, the Public Health Act 1848 was the first attempt at national legislation for the control of the environmental effects of waste. It was this Act which created the term 'statutory nuisance' which refers, amongst other things, to any accumulation or deposit which is prejudicial to health or is a nuisance. The Act gave local government authorities the power to act on behalf of the public.

Public Health Act 1936 (part still in force)

A series of Acts, similar to the Public Health Act 1848, culminated in the Public Health Act of 1936 which consolidated the previous legislation. In general terms this Act gave local authorities the powers to police and inspect waste arisings in their area, to remove or require the removal of waste and to prosecute offenders.

More specifically, the Act gave local authorities power to remove house and trade refuse and to require the removal of 'any accumulation of noxious matter'. It imposed a duty on local authorities to inspect their areas for 'statutory nuisance' and gave subsequent power to serve abatement notices and prosecute offenders.

Town and Country Planning Act 1947 (superseded)

The first measures to prevent the potentially damaging environmental effects of waste, rather than to clean up afterwards, were included in this Act. The Act required that any new development, including waste disposal sites and plants, should have planning permission.

Town and Country Planning Act 1971 (as amended) (superseded)

This Act superseded the Town and Country Planning Act 1947, and controlled the use of land for waste disposal through:

(a) Structure plans which set out the policies and general proposals for the development and other use of the land;
(b) Local plans which relate the policies of the structure plan to precise areas of land; and
(c) The granting or refusal of planning permission.

The equivalent Scottish legislation, the Town and Country Planning (Scotland) Act 1972, achieved the same objectives.

Deposit of Poisonous Waste Act 1972 (superseded)

An incident arising from the casual tipping of cyanide wastes in the industrial Midlands of England was the first and best known in a series of well-publicized incidents relating to the tipping of toxic wastes. This occurred prior to the drafting of Part I of the Control of Pollution Act and, whilst this drafting was in progress, interim emergency legislation was rushed through Parliament in response to public pressure for tighter controls in this area. This legislation was the Deposit of Poisonous Waste Act 1972 and, although intended to be an interim measure, was only repealed in 1981 after the implementation in 1980 of the Control of Pollution (Special Waste) Regulations 1980.

The 1972 Act was intended to 'penalize the depositing on land of poisonous, noxious or polluting wastes so as to give rise to an environmental hazard, and to make offenders liable for any resultant damage; to require the giving of notices in connection with the removal or deposit of waste, and for connected purposes'. For a waste to be considered as potentially giving rise to a hazard it has to be present in sufficient concentration or quantity to threaten death or injury to persons or animals or, alternatively, to threaten to contaminate a surface or underground water supply.

In order to monitor the movement of 'poisonous, noxious or polluting wastes', the Act established a notification procedure whereby local government and regional water authorities had to be notified both in the area from which the waste was removed and the area in which it was to be deposited. The notification procedure was applied on the exclusion principal, i.e. it applied to every waste with the exception of those listed in the Act or deposited in a manner detailed by the Act. For all wastes not listed in the Act, the notices had to specify:

(i)   The premises from which it was to be removed and the land on which it was to be deposited;
(ii) The nature and chemical composition;
(iii) The quantity to be removed or deposited, together with details of the number, size and description of any containers, and
(iv) The name of the person who was to undertake the removal.

Control of Pollution Act 1974 (COPA 1974) (part still in force)

Part 1 of the Control of Pollution Act (COPA) 1974 was intended to provide legislation for a systematic and co-ordinated approach to waste collection and disposal. With certain specified exemptions, the Act gave control to local (waste disposal) authorities of wastes arising from household, industrial, trade and commercial premises. These wastes were hereafter referred to as 'controlled wastes'. (It should be noted that the definition of 'controlled wastes' altered with the implementation of the Environmental Protection Act 1990).

Waste disposal authorities were required by the 1974 Act to draw up and regularly review a plan for the disposal of all controlled wastes. The plan should include information about:

1. The kinds and quantities of waste which would arise in the area, or be brought into it, during the period of the plan;
2. What waste the authority expected to dispose of itself;
3. What waste others were expected to dispose of;
4. The methods of disposal, e.g. reclamation, incineration, landfill;
5. The sites and equipment being provided; and
6. The cost.

The authorities were also required to consider what steps might reasonably be taken to reclaim and recycle waste materials.

A further major requirement of the Act was that a site should be licensed before it could be used for the treatment or disposal of controlled waste. The licence was additional to the planning permission which was required under the Town and Country

Planning Act 1971, although it could only be refused if the authority was satisfied that its refusal was necessary for preventing pollution or danger to public health. All current site licences were kept on a public register, and the authority had a duty to supervise licensed activities.

Dumping at Sea Act 1974 (superseded)

Former voluntary schemes covering nearly all industrial waste and sewage sludges were formally implemented by the Dumping at Sea Act 1974. This Act made it an offence to dump, or to load for the purpose of dumping, any material in UK waters or from a UK ship, vehicle, hovercraft or marine structure without a licence from the relevant licensing authority. The licensing authority was required by the Act to 'have regard to the need to protect the marine environment and the living resources which it supports from any adverse consequence of dumping'. The term 'Dumping at Sea' included incineration at sea.

Refuse Disposal (Amenity) Act 1978 (still in force)

This Act places a duty on local authorities to provide sites ('civic amenity sites') to which their residents may bring bulky household refuse free of charge.

Control of Pollution (Special Waste) Regulations 1980 (still in force)

These special regulations for the control of wastes which are particularly hazardous or difficult to deal with were made under Section 17 of COPA 1974 and replaced many of the provisions made in the Deposit of Poisonous Waste Act 1972. Whilst the 1972 Act operated on the 'exclusive' basis, the Section 17 Regulations operate on an 'inclusive' basis, controlling a newly-defined category of wastes called 'special wastes'. These controls are principally aimed at protecting public health rather than the environment. The environment was felt to be adequately protected by provisions in other Sections of the 1974 Act, namely by control of site licence conditions and of discharges to water.

Waste is 'special' if it is a medicinal product available only on prescription or if it contains any of the substances listed in a schedule of the Regulations in such concentrations as to have:

I.   The ability to be likely to cause death or serious damage to tissue if a single dose of not more than $5cm^3$ was to be ingested by a child of 20kg body weight; or
II. The ability to be likely to cause serious damage to human tissue by inhalation, skin contact or eye contact on exposure to the substance for 15 minutes or less; or
III. A flash point of 21°C or less.

The Regulations provide for a 'cradle to grave' control system for the disposal of special wastes. A consignment system has been set up, and waste producers are required to inform receiving waste disposal authorities of their intention to dispose of special wastes. Compliance with the consignment system requires a record to be kept of the dispatch, conveyance and disposal of the waste, with a permanent record being retained at the place of ultimate disposal.

Food and Environment Protection Act 1985 (still in force)

Part II of the Food and Environment Protection Act 1985 supersedes the Dumping at Sea Act 1974, but provides similar legislative control.

Control of Pollution (Amendment) Act 1989

This legislation came into force under the Controlled Waste (Registration of Carriers and Seizure of Vehicles) Regulations 1991 and provides for the registration of carriers of controlled waste.

Town and Country Planning Act 1990 (still in force)

The 1990 Act abolished the requirement for structure plans introduced by the Town and Country Planning Act 1971. However, the main provisions in respect of wastes management were inserted by the Planning and Compensation Act 1991, effective from February 1992.

Applying only to non-metropolitan areas, this legislation introduced a requirement for planning authorities to prepare a waste local plan for their area and to include their waste policies in their minerals local plan.

Implementation of the Waste Framework Directive (75/442/EEC) under the Waste Management Licensing Regulations 1994 required local authorities to ensure protection of the environment when considering applications for the recovery or disposal of waste.

Environmental Protection Act 1990 (EPA 1990) (still in force)

When fully in force in relation to waste on land, this Act will replace:

- the provisions of the Control of Pollution Act 1974;
- the law defining statutory nuisances;
- the law relating to litter;

will make further provision for:

- the importation and exportation of certain wastes;

will amend the law relating to the control of hazardous substances;

and will amend:

- the Food and Environment Protection Act 1985 regarding the dumping of waste at sea.

Sections of the legislation relating to waste on land (Part II of the 1990 Act), that have been implemented include those defining controlled wastes and those regarding Waste Management Licensing (1994), litter, statutory nuisances, the Duty of Care (1992) and waste recycling credits.

Controlled wastes are defined under Section 75 of the Environmental Protection Act 1990 and further in the Controlled Waste Regulations 1992 (SI 1992. No. 588) as 'household, industrial and commercial waste or any such waste' (i.e. which may be inferred to be such waste).

The definition of waste in Section 75 has been modified by the Waste Management Licensing Regulations 1994 to include reference to waste as defined in the 1975 EC Framework Directive on Waste (as amended in 1991). UK guidance (DoE 11/94) suggests that waste now be defined as 'those substances which fall out of the commercial cycle or out of the chain of utility'.

The government has brought into force the legislation for waste recycling payments (recycling credits) to encourage local authorities in the pursuance of the recycling of household waste. The objective of this legislation is to make available to recyclers the savings in collection and disposal costs which result from recycling household wastes.

The Duty of Care and the Waste Management Licensing Regulations are described in the next chapter.

EC Legislation

There are a number of EC Directives on Wastes Management. These are listed in Table I, and have generally been implemented in the UK under COPA 1974 (and, more specifically, under the Control of Pollution (Special Waste) Regulations 1980) and the Environmental Protection Act 1990.

COPA 1974 lays down particular requirements for the protection of ground and surface waters. Groundwaters are protected from the polluting effects of waste disposal by EEC Directive 80/68 which was implemented in the UK under COPA 1974 and the Water Resources Act 1991. This Directive has appended List I and List II of

Table I. EC legislation on wastes management

No	Description	Formal compliance in UK
75/439/EEC	Council Directive on the disposal of waste oils	
75/442/EEC	Directive on waste	July 1977 under COPA; actually implemented July 1978
76/403/EEC	Directive on the disposal of polychlorinated biphenyls and polychlorinated terphenyls	1981 under COPA 1974 Section 17 Regs
78/319/EEC	Directive on toxic and dangerous waste	22 March 1980 under COPA and 1981 under Section 17 (Special Waste Regs)
80/68/EEC	Directive on the protection of groundwater against pollution caused by certain dangerous substances	COPA 1974 (legislation already in place)
84/631/EEC	Directive on the supervision and control within the European Community of the transfrontier shipment of hazardous waste	1994 under Control of Pollution (Amendment) Act 1989
85/469/EEC	Adaptation of 84/631/EEC (Commission Directive)	
86/278/EEC	Directive on the protection of the environment and in particular of the soil, when sewage sludge is used in agriculture	19 June 1989
89/369/EEC	Directive on air pollution from new municipal waste incinerators	Implemented under the EPA 1990
89/429/EEC	Directive on air pollution from existing municipal waste incinerators	– ditto –
COM(91)102	Draft Directive regulating the landfill of waste	
COM(91)21	Draft Directive on civil liability for damage caused by waste	
91/156/EEC	Directive amending 75/442/EEC on waste	

91/689/EEC	Directive on hazardous waste
COM(92)9 Final	Proposal for a Council Directive on the incineration of hazardous waste
COM(92)278 Final	Draft Directive on packaging and packaging waste
94/3/EC	Commission Decision on a list of wastes

families and groups of dangerous substances, those on List I generally being more dangerous than those on List II. The Directive requires the prevention of List I substances from, and a limit to the quantity of List II substances, entering groundwater. All direct discharges of List I substances are to be prohibited, although if after investigation the groundwater is found to be unsuitable for other uses, such discharges may be authorized.

At the time of writing, consideration of the proposed Directive regulating the landfill of waste continues, although there is now a common position for the harmonizing of technical and environmental norms for landfills across the European Union. Individual Member States have considerable latitude to develop national policy in line with the overall framework of the proposed Directive. A key issue for the UK was that co-disposal should be permitted to continue and this will be the case, subject to conditions which are to be met by Member States using co-disposal within five years of the Directive coming into force. Existing landfills or those created between 1994 and the adoption of the Directive must meet the required standards within ten years of adoption, or close. The text of the common position suggests a categorization of wastes as dangerous, non-dangerous or inert, with required procedures for disposal dependent upon the relevant category. The common position has been adopted under the co-operation procedure and the text has now to be placed before the European Parliament.

ADVICE TO GOVERNMENT

Government Working Groups

As a result of public concern in the 1960s about the environmental effect of wastes, two government working groups were set up to examine the issue in more detail than formerly. The first committee, the Key Committee, was set up in 1964 to examine toxic waste; the second, the Sumner Committee, in 1967 to examine refuse disposal. The reports of these two committees influenced the drafting of Part I of the Control of

Pollution Act 1974 which deals extensively with both domestic and industrial waste. The House of Commons Select Committee on the Environment completed their inquiry on the subject of toxic waste in 1989.

The Royal Commission on Environmental Pollution

The Royal Commission was appointed on 20 February 1970 as a standing body to advise on matters national and international concerning pollution of the environment, on the adequacy of research in this field and the future possibilities of danger to the environment.

Since 1971, they have published eighteen reports on environmental pollution. Three of particular relevance to waste are the 11th report: *Managing Waste: The Duty of Care* the 12th report: *Best Practicable Environmental Option* and the 17th report: *Incineration of Waste*. The 11th report introduced the concept of cradle-to-grave responsibility for waste — later enshrined in the Environmental Protection Act 1990. The 17th report caused considerable interest as it advocated incineration of waste as an acceptable environmental option. This was at a time when many planning applications for incinerators were being refused because of the inability of both the public and planners to consider them environmentally acceptable.

NATIONAL REGULATORY AGENCIES

Her Majesty's Inspectorate of Pollution

In 1986 the UK Government established a unified Pollution Inspectorate for England and Wales: Her Majesty's Inspectorate of Pollution (HMIP). The inspectorate was required to develop a more coherent approach to the control of industrial emissions to air, water or land and to provide advice which would help the other pollution control authorities to carry out their statutory responsibilities. This Inspectorate comprised the former Alkali Inspectorate, the Hazardous Waste Inspectorate (formed in 1981 to examine and make recommendations for the management of hazardous waste) and the then newly-formed Water Directorate (responsible for discharges to water). It should be noted that, whereas the Hazardous Waste Inspectorate concerned itself only with hazardous wastes, HMIP is required to examine the management of all controlled wastes.

The Environment Agency

In the 1993 Queen's speech to Parliament, the government announced its intention to set up a new agency dealing with all aspects of environmental protection, to be known as the Environment Agency.

At the time of writing, the Agency will comprise HMIP (excluding the Drinking Water

Directorate), the National Rivers Authority and the newly-formed Waste Regulation Authorities (WRAs). In Scotland, the equivalent body is the Scottish Environmental Protection Agency, formed from Her Majesty's Industrial Pollution Inspectorate, the River Purification Authorities, the waste regulation sections of the district councils and the local authority air pollution functions.

The new authorities are due to come into existence early in 1997.

EFFECTS ON UK PRACTICE

Landfill practice in the UK has altered considerably, particularly as a result of the Deposit of Poisonous Waste Act 1972, COPA 1974 and EPA 1990 (see described above). This has resulted in restrictions on the types of wastes that can be placed in landfill sites, and has allowed local authorities a means (through planning and site licence consents) of further control. Thus the types of wastes and manner of placing, together with environmental aspects such as landfill gas and leachate control, and eventual site restoration can all be stipulated by the local authority. The waste producer has an ongoing responsibility to ensure the proper disposal of his wastes. The waste management licence holder has to ensure protection of the environment from his operation and show that financial provision has been made to remedy any environmental damage which may result.

The restrictions currently placed on a landfill site operation mean that, prior to applying for planning permission or a site licence, it is incumbent upon the proposed operator of the site to carry out a full site investigation and engineering design. The site investigation should particularly identify any potential geological pathways for pollutants such as fissures or permeable and porous strata. The engineering design should take account of the potential of waste to produce pollutants, and should aim to limit their production and control their eventual discharge into the environment. The Landfill Directive is likely to require the lining of all sites except those accepting only totally inert material.

All leachate discharges to groundwater, surface and marine waters are controlled under the Water Resources Act 1991 (England and Wales). There is thus a control on the type and quantity of pollutants which can enter any watercourse, and the opportunity for local authorities to prohibit any such discharge if it is deemed appropriate. This has resulted in the increasing use of contained (i.e. naturally or artificially impermeably lined) sites, limiting discharges to groundwater, and of the practice of collecting and treating leachate, limiting discharges to surface waters.

Fly tipping, i.e. the unwanted, indiscriminate dumping of wastes, is a practice which has been a problem in the UK for centuries. Each successive Act aimed at curbing the damaging environmental effects of waste management has sought to control fly tipping. Whilst it is still difficult to apprehend the casual fly tipper, current legislation requiring registration of carriers and a transfer note to accompany the waste showing that it has been passed on to a suitably responsible person should reduce this problem.

With a growing shortage of landfill sites in locations which are convenient for waste disposal, increasing use is being made in the UK of technologies such as incineration and pulverization/shredding and the production of refuse-derived fuels. A wide variety of further legislative controls exist for these operations, but will not be detailed here except to note that all these operations require planning permission and waste management licences.

3. MAJOR CURRENT LEGISLATION

INTRODUCTION

There has been a significant change, during the early 1990s, in the regulation of waste management activities. The introduction in 1994 of Planning Policy Guidance Note 23 on Pollution Control relates specifically to the need to consider pollution arising from waste disposal. The Duty of Care and Waste Management Licensing Regulations, brought into force under the Environmental Protection Act 1990 and the Registration of Carriers Regulations brought in under the Control of Pollution (Amendment) Act 1989, mean that the local regulatory authority should now be notified about and have control over all waste management activities in its area. These regulations contribute substantially to the advancement of the government's policy that the polluter should pay for environmental damage caused by his activities.

WASTE DISPOSAL PLANS

Since August 1991, Waste Collection Authorities (WCAs) have been required (under Section 49 of the Environmental Protection Act 1990) to prepare a recycling plan in the form of a statement giving information about the quantities and types of wastes they intend to recycle and the methods they propose to use. Costs or savings attributable to the methods proposed should be stated. Plans should be well publicized and available for public inspection, and should be periodically reviewed and modified.

Since May 1991, Waste Regulation Authorities (WRAs) have been required (under Section 50 of the Environmental Protection Act 1990) to formulate a plan in the form of a statement for the treatment or disposal of controlled waste likely to arise in their areas. The plan should specify arisings (including imports and exports to the area) and methods of treatment and disposal. The public should be made aware of the plan and given the opportunity to make representations about it. The plan should be periodically reviewed and updated.

From May 1994, Section 67 of the Environmental Protection Act 1990 requires WRAs to prepare annual reports containing information about their licensing and enforcing activities, the implementation of their waste plans (as described above) and the cost of carrying out their duties.

PLANNING APPLICATIONS

Under the Town and Country Planning Acts (see Chapter 2) it has been a requirement since 1947 that any waste facility must have planning permission. This includes transfer stations, treatment plants, recycling plants, civic amenity sites and disposal sites. In this booklet incinerators are considered to be treatment plants. Refuse-derived fuel plants (production and use) also require planning permission.

A planning application will be considered by the local planning authority in whose area the proposed site lies. In England this is a county authority, in Wales a district authority, and in Scotland the district, regional or island authority. In England, the application may have to be submitted to the district or borough planning office for the site area, and will then be passed to the county planning authority for consideration. In the former metropolitan areas, the district authority (in London, the borough council) considers the application. In Scotland, all planning applications are dealt with by the district council, except in Highland, Dumfries and Galloway and the Borders Regional Councils. In these areas, applications are considered by the region as there is no district planning function.

The application, which should be made on a form supplied by the planning authority, should be accompanied by a statement and drawings identifying the site and outlining the proposed operation. The appropriate fee should also be submitted (unless the application is made by a public authority).

There is significant variation in the amount of detail required by the planning authorities across the country. Although some will only require a simple form stating the type of application with the barest information relating to the operation, others will require full details including the type and number of vehicles to be used on site (e.g. for a landfill operation). It is in the interests of the applicant that all relevant planning matters, i.e. those related to land use, are addressed. Aspects such as the adequacy of proposals to deal with the phasing of operations and restoration (in the case of a landfill) or architecture and landscaping (in the case of a structure) can be important factors for consideration by the local authority. It should be noted that although the control and management of leachate and landfill gas are more appropriately regulated under the licensing regime, many planning authorities will wish to be satisfied as to the adequacy of the proposals under the precautionary principle.

Guidance on the relevance of pollution controls in relation to the planning function is given, for the first time, in Planning Policy Guidance Note 23 published in July 1994. The document provides a useful précis of the environmental law in force at the time of its publication and makes particular reference to applications for waste management facilities (in compliance with the EC Framework Directive on Waste). Specific guidance is given for landfill and incinerator applications.

Since July 1988, it has also been a legal requirement that an environmental statement accompanies certain planning applications pertaining to waste disposal. The DoE Circular (15/88) giving guidance on the requirements for environmental assessment advises that an environmental statement may only be required for waste disposal facilities receiving in excess of 75 000 tonnes per year. However, the sensitive and emotive nature of development associated with waste disposal facilities has led many waste operators to volunteer an environmental statement to allay public concern, even when this is not strictly required by the planning regulations.

Consultations with interested parties are made by the planning authority whilst considering the application. Interested parties include the National Rivers Authority (NRA) in England and Wales, the River Purification Authority (RPA) in Scotland, English Nature or Scottish National Heritage, Heritage Trust or Historic Scotland and others, as appropriate. If valuable mineral deposits lie beneath the site, the owner of the land or of the rights of the deposit will also be consulted.

DUTY OF CARE

Known as the Duty of Care, this major new piece of legislation came into force in April 1992 under Section 34 of the Environmental Protection Act 1990. The regulations (SI 1991. No. 2839) require all who are involved in dealing with controlled waste to take reasonable steps to prevent anyone else illegally treating or disposing of it and to prevent its unauthorized escape. The DoE have issued a guidance note on the Duty of Care (Circular 19/91), which includes a Code of Practice.

The Code of Practice suggests criteria against which waste may be defined:

- what would ordinarily be described as waste;
- a scrap material;
- an effluent or other unwanted surplus substance;
- it requires to be disposed of as broken, worn out, contaminated or otherwise spoiled;
- it is being discarded or dealt with as if it were waste.

The Duty of Care requires such materials only to be treated, kept or disposed of in accordance with a waste management licence or in such a way that it is not likely to cause pollution of the environment or harm to human health.

The regulations introduce a transfer note system to ensure that waste is only handed over to an authorized person (generally a registered carrier or someone holding a waste management licence). The transfer note must contain an adequate description of the waste and travels with the waste. The parties involved in each transaction of the waste to its final disposal are required to sign the note, to demonstrate that they have passed the waste only to a suitably authorized person. The intention of this regulation was to make producers of waste responsible for the safe management and disposal of that waste. Breach of the Duty is a criminal offence.

The only persons exempted from the Duty of Care are occupiers of household property in respect of their own household waste.

REGISTRATION OF CARRIERS

Under the Control of Pollution (Amendment) Act 1989, all carriers of controlled waste are required (from 1 April, 1992) to be authorized and registered. Officers of the WRA, accompanied always by a policeman, may stop a carrier at any time, search the vehicle, take samples for testing and require the carrier to show his authorization.

WASTE MANAGEMENT LICENCES

A significant amendment to the regulation of waste management facilities has been brought about by the implementation in 1994 of the Waste Licensing Regulations. Brought into force under the Environmental Protection Act 1990, these regulations require all facilities for the storage, treatment or disposal of wastes to be licensed. These regulations apply equally to mobile and permanent plant. Activities exempt from licensing (of which there are many) must be registered with the local WRA.

Licences may only be held by 'fit and proper persons', i.e. those who: (a) have not been convicted of a relevant offence, (b) have made adequate financial provision for remedying any environmental damage which may result from their site, and (c) can show that the management of the activities will be in the hands of a technically competent person.

Under these regulations, the application for the licence must be accompanied by a working plan showing how the site is intended to be operated and what precautions will be taken to minimize damage to the environment or harm to human health. Specific aspects which should be covered include the types of wastes and rate of disposal, the control of leachate and gas, the protection of particularly sensitive natural resources (e.g. a Site of Special Scientific Interest), the method of filling, records which will be kept and how restoration and after-care will be carried out.

The licence can only be handed back to the WRA when that Authority is satisfied that the facility is unlikely to cause damage to the environment or harm to human health, now, or in the future, by reason of the licensed activity. When the Authority is satisfied on this issue, a certificate of completion will be issued and the licence rescinded.

CERTIFICATE OF TECHNICAL COMPETENCE

Before a waste management licence can be granted, the potential licence holder must be able to show that the manager of the facility holds a relevant Certificate of Technical Competence (COTC). Certificates are issued by the Waste Management Industries' Training and Advisory Board (WAMITAB). An applicant's competence is assessed on the accumulation of National Vocational Qualifications (NVQs) and the level of these required for a particular facility. For instance, a person holding a COTC for a landfill site taking only inert wastes is not considered competent to hold a licence for a hazardous waste facility. Conversely, a holder of a COTC for a landfill taking hazardous wastes would be considered competent to run a facility for the disposal of inert wastes.

DISPOSAL AT SEA

The disposal of waste at sea also requires a licence which is issued by the Ministry of Agriculture, Fisheries and Food (MAFF) or the Department of Agriculture and Fisheries for Scotland (DAFS) under the Food and Environment Protection Act 1985. The North Sea Treaty required the dumping of liquid industrial wastes to end by 1992, the termination of marine incineration by 1994 and the dumping of sewage sludge to be phased out by 1998. Under the Environmental Protection Act 1990 the licensing authorities are required to keep a public register of licences for the deposit or incineration of waste at sea.

4. WASTE ARISINGS

INTRODUCTION

The magnitude of the problem associated with the management of waste materials only really becomes apparent on examination of the actual volumes or tonnages of these materials which are produced each year. Per head of population, about 0.3 tonnes of household waste are discarded every year. This means that each person discards the equivalent weight of 300, one kilogramme bags of sugar per year. When it is realized that there are about 58 million people in the UK, the size of the task can begin to be imagined.

The UK Waste Management System

Household, most commercial and some industrial wastes are collected by the district WCAs or by privatized companies under their management. The disposal of these wastes is managed by the Waste Disposal Authority (WDA) – at county level in England and Wales and district level elsewhere. Until 1992, many WDAs in England and Wales actually carried out the function of disposal. However, in 1991, Section 32 of the Environmental Protection Act 1990 came into force in England and Wales, requiring the WDAs to set up private waste disposal companies to carry out the function of disposal. Known as Local Authority Waste Disposal Companies (LAWDCs), the first one was vested by the Secretary of State in 1992. The purpose of this exercise was to separate out the function of disposal from the regulation and policing of that disposal. Out of the former (pre-1991) waste disposal authority, there are now three bodies:

(I)   the new Waste Disposal Authority whose function is to manage contracts for the disposal of waste and to manage landfill sites not transferred to LAWDCs;

(II) the LAWDC which, whilst it may be wholly or partially owned by the local authority or an independent company, tenders competitively in the market place for waste disposal contracts; and

(III) the WRA which, at county level, issues and enforces licences and generally polices waste disposal activities. London has a unique waste regulatory body — the London Waste Regulation Authority (LWRA) — which carries out these functions. At the time of writing, it is proposed that the WRAs and the LWRA form part of the government's new Environment Agency.

Wastes other than those described above are managed by private contractors in privately owned facilities. These activities are licensed and policed by the WRAs.

In Scotland and Northern Ireland, the waste regulation and disposal function has remained with the district councils, although in Northern Ireland, central government plays an important role in regulation.

ARISINGS

Of the categories considered in this publication (excluding agricultural and radioactive wastes) there were 255 million tonnes of waste generated in 1990 in the UK (Figure 1). Of this, about 20 million tonnes were household arisings, about 2.5 million tonnes were defined as special and the remainder was mine and quarry, commercial, construction and demolition waste, non-special industrial waste and sewage sludge. In addition to those wastes generated in the UK, some 44 000 tonnes of hazardous wastes were imported for treatment at UK facilities.

Controlled Wastes

The WCAs and WDAs described above manage the collection and disposal of the majority (i.e. all household, some commercial and a little industrial) of controlled wastes. All controlled wastes are policed by the WRAs. The most recent figures available[1] show that during 1986/87, English and Welsh waste disposal authorities handled about 27 million tonnes, while during 1989, 8.7 million tonnes of controlled waste were disposed of in Scotland. The remainder (see Figure 1) is handled by private contractors.

Household Wastes

The term household wastes includes waste from households, caravans on caravan sites, residential homes, university or other halls of residence, school boarding houses, and parts of hospitals and nursing homes. Some 20 million tonnes are produced each year.

Commercial Wastes

Commercial wastes are those which arise generally from premises used wholly or

---

[1]Waste Management Paper 1, 1992

mainly for the purposes of a trade or business, or for the purposes of sport, recreation or entertainment and amounted to approximately 15 million tonnes in 1990.

Industrial Wastes
This category includes waste from a wide variety of sources, but is estimated to include 47.5 million tonnes of general industrial waste, 32 million tonnes of demolition and construction building waste and about 13 million tonnes of power station waste.

Hazardous Wastes
About 44 000 tonnes of hazardous wastes were imported into England and Wales in 1990, for treatment and disposal in the UK. In the same year, about 180 tonnes were imported into Scotland.

Special Wastes
Statistics on special waste arisings for 1986/87 to 1990/91 are given in the *Digest of Environmental Protection and Water Statistics. No. 14*, 1991. The figures are subject to considerable fluctuation and error due to the poor response from local authorities in supplying the data, and the nature of contaminated soil arisings which contribute to this statistic. However, the figures indicate that for 1990/91, some 2.4 million tonnes of special wastes arose in England, 76 000 tonnes in Wales, 94 000 tonnes in Scotland and 20 000 tonnes in Northern Ireland.

Non-Controlled Wastes

Mine and Quarry Wastes
About 107 million tonnes of mining wastes and quarry wastes are produced each year of which 50 million tonnes are colliery and slate wastes, 27 million tonnes are china clay wastes and 30 million tonnes are from quarrying activities (excluding open-cast coal mining).

Sewage Sludge
Some 25 million tonnes of sewage sludge are produced annually at sewage treatment works in the UK. The water content varies between 95 and 98 per cent, and the overall dry solids content is estimated at one million tonnes. It should be noted that sewage sludge is now quoted as weight of dry solids in order to eliminate confusion when making comparison with tonnages of other solid wastes.

Agricultural Wastes
About 250 million tonnes of agricultural wastes are produced each year, including manures and straw arising from animal bedding.

Radioactive Wastes

Statistics of radioactive waste arisings have been compiled by the Nuclear Industry Radioactive Waste Executive (Nirex) and published in a summary report entitled *Radioactive Waste Arisings in the UK*. This provides an estimate of all low and intermediate-level wastes to the year 2030 and some decommissioning wastes beyond 2030, and includes all existing stocks and projected arisings. Estimated volumes for disposal[2] to 2030 are 300 000m^3 of intermediate and 500 000m^3 of low-level wastes. Of these volumes, 80 000m^3 of the intermediate and 250 000m^3 of the low-level wastes are postulated to result from decommissioning. A proportion of this waste is likely to be disposed of at the British Nuclear Fuel site at Drigg.

IMPORTS AND EXPORTS

All WDAs may permit the import and export of waste to facilitate the best and most cost-effective method of disposal. In general, this practice is confined to movements within the UK mainland. It is self-evident that waste, particularly household and commercial which is generated in the large metropolitan areas must, to a great extent, be disposed of outside those areas. Special wastes are exported to the county with the best facilities for their treatment or disposal. The Hazardous Waste Inspectorate's Third Report, published in June 1988, gives details of special waste imports and exports for each county. No further details have been published since that date.

In addition to movement of waste within the UK, some waste is imported into the country for treatment and disposal. So far, wastes imported to the UK have been restricted to hazardous wastes for which there are good treatment and disposal facilities. For certain wastes, this practice should be continued, and indeed encouraged, as the imported quantities are necessary to make hazardous waste incinerators commercially viable and they generate income for UK companies. However, because the environmental laws governing the disposal of certain wastes to landfill are more relaxed in the UK than in certain of our European neighbours, some of the imported waste currently goes, untreated, to landfill. This practice does not help to support the country's hazardous-waste facilities, uses up valuable landfill space and should be discouraged. Recently there have been moves by private enterprise to import household wastes (principally from USA) and hazardous wastes (principally from Germany) for landfill in the UK. This proposal caused such a public outcry that the government was required to take steps to prevent it being carried out.

---

[2]*Note: These estimates differ from those published elsewhere by the DoE, which suggest there may be one million cubic metres of low level wastes, 200 000m^3 of intermediate level wastes and 3500m^3 of high level wastes.*

5. TREATMENT AND TRANSPORT

INTRODUCTION

The principal reasons for treating waste are to make it easier to transport and dispose of, and to facilitate resource recovery. Therefore for most wastes (household, commercial and some industrial), the main aims are: (a) to reduce bulk, (b) to reduce the costs of transportation, and (c) to prolong the life of disposal facilities. For hazardous and special wastes the objective is to reduce their hazardous nature, both with regard to human contact in the short term and to protect the environment in the long term.

Environmental and economic pressures (mainly the former) and the government's target to recycle 25 per cent of household waste by the year 2000[1], have led to increased efforts to promote the recovery and reuse of as much of the resources as possible. This includes recovery of material (tin, glass, etc.) segregated by the consumer/producer from the bulk of waste prior to disposal, recovery of by-products from industrial processes, and minimizing the use of fossil fuels through heat exchange, district heating and refuse-derived fuel. The government has introduced a payment for recycling waste (known as Recycling Credits) to encourage recycling (DoE Circular 4/92). Not all these efforts have been successful, as may be seen in the later sections of this chapter.

The proportions of household waste treated for volume reduction or resource recovery are shown in Table II.

---

[1] *This Common Inheritance Cm 1200, 1990.*

Table II. Methods of treatment and disposal of municipal wastes (1988-89)

	Per cent by weight
Landfill disposal without treatment	79
Incineration	6
Compaction/shredding/baling	13
Reclamation and other methods	2

RESOURCE RECOVERY

Recycling

The average composition of household waste is given in Table III, and various constituents (including heat generated by burning) can be recovered from the waste streams. Recently there has been significant pressure to recover and reuse the various constituents of waste. This has arisen from: (a) environment lobbyists who wish to minimize the use of mineral and other finite resources, (b) the European Union (see Chapter 2), (c) the government's target for recycling household waste, and (d) the fact that in certain parts of the country WRAs are exploring any avenue which will prolong the life of traditional disposal routes such as landfill. The WCAs and WDAs are, therefore, promoting any exercise which will reduce the volume of waste for disposal. However, largely due to the lack of reliable markets for recycled products, less than 5 per cent of the 20 million tonnes per year of household waste arisings has been recycled over the past few years and this figure has recently dropped to 3.8 per cent (1993).

Table III. Composition of average household waste in UK (data from a variety of sources)

	As collected per cent by weight
* Paper	29
Vegetable/putrescible	23
* Ferrous metals	8
* Glass	8
* Non-ferrous metals	1
* Textiles	3
Rubber/leather/wood	8
* Plastics	7
Fines/dust/ash	13

*These constituents are potentially recoverable. Moisture content of household waste is generally about 25 per cent by weight.

Once the various constituents of waste are mixed in a dustbin, it becomes expensive to separate out materials which can be recycled. An experimental plant was constructed in Doncaster in 1980, to separate out such materials after they have been mixed. This trial plant was the most comprehensive of its kind in the UK and could separate out tin, aluminium, glass (and separate this into colours) and ceramics. However, it proved not to be commercially viable and closed in 1986.

It is much easier to recover materials if they are kept separate by the consumer/producer, i.e. if glass, tin, etc., are never mixed or cross-contaminated but are disposed of by their own separate routes. There are currently three systems available for the segregation of household wastes: (a) 'bring systems' where facilities are provided at supermarkets and other locations visited regularly by householders, in which they may deposit recyclable wastes; (b) 'collect systems' where materials are segregated by householders into various categories for doorstep or kerb-side collection and (c) 'centralized segregation' where materials are segregated into different categories after collection (see above) usually associated with energy recovery from those fractions which are not segregated:

(i) *Glass.* Bottle banks are now a familiar sight in most parts of the country. Sponsored jointly by the British Glass Federation and the WDAs, the bottle banks save the British Glass Federation thousands of tonnes of oil per annum, and also save the WDAs a proportion of their waste disposal costs;

(ii) *Cans.* During the last 10 years there have been several schemes to recycle tin cans. Some have been aimed at recovering tin and steel, some at recovering aluminium; however, not all have been successful. The most notable recent ones have been Save-a-Can, Cash-a-Can and Vend-a-Can. As may be anticipated, the last two operate on a cash-back system;

(iii) *Paper.* Recovery of paper, which is a fluctuating fashion, became popular in the early seventies when environmental consciousness was first being raised. About 17 trees are required to produce 1 tonne of paper and, although this is not a finite resource, people become concerned about the felling of woodlands and forests and the destruction of natural habitats. In the UK, local authorities would collect waste paper (i.e. bundles of newspapers etc.) separately for recycling. However, in 1974 there was a recession in this market and some councils were literally left with fields full of bundles of waste paper awaiting reuse. For about a decade, recycling of used waste paper (as opposed to clean factory waste paper) has continued slowly. Some WCAs are again collecting waste paper and board separately: however, the market has been and is, extremely cyclical and is currently flooded by imports of waste paper from the USA and Germany;

(iv) *Plastics.* From the packaging of nearly all consumer products, it would appear that there are large amounts of plastics available for recycling. Unfortunately, these materials are made by a variety of processes which are not always compatible with each other. Therefore, not only do such materials have to be discarded separately from other waste, they have to be separated out according to the original manufacturing process: this tends to discourage their collection. However, there is a process for collecting and recycling polyethylene tetrafluoride containers, i.e. those containing carbonated drinks, and some supermarkets provide receptacles for such containers.

The government gives such importance to the recycling of wastes that they have introduced recycling credits and have prepared general guidance on the subject in the form of a Waste Management Paper (No. 28). At the time of writing, the government has just announced the introduction of a tax on disposal by landfill, possibly designed to enhance the viability of recycling (i.e. to make it more attractive financially when compared with the cost of landfill) and to encourage more wastes to be managed through this route. However, the viability of recycling will always be governed by the availability of markets for the recycled product and, except for glass, these continue to be uncertain.

Refuse-Derived Fuel

The production of refuse-derived fuel (RDF) is more a method of recovering resources from waste than of reducing the volume of waste for disposal. RDF refers to the use of both the organic constituents of waste and plastics for the production of energy by burning. Therefore, prior to its use, some sort of separation process, such as shredding or pulverization, must occur. Only about 40 per cent of controlled waste is suitable for RDF production and there is always a residue which requires disposal.

During the last 15–20 years, research into the use of RDF has progressed significantly and, as there are still many problems associated with its use, its current viability in the UK is uncertain. It is now possible to burn loose pulverized or crushed waste on a coal-type moving grate, with or without coal. Alternatively, the waste can be made into briquettes or pellets which can be stored satisfactorily and burned, again with or without coal. Methods are now available for enhancing the calorific value of RDF (untreated, at about two-thirds that of coal), one of which is by the addition of an oil — itself derived from waste.

Energy From Waste

It has been estimated that the household, industrial and agricultural wastes generated annually in the UK have a potential energy value equivalent to 30 million tonnes of coal (around 10 per cent of the UK's primary energy requirement); only about 1.5 per cent of this potential is currently utilized. The government is keen to encourage the use of renewable sources of energy and has introduced the Non-Fossil Fuel Obligation (NFFO) under the Electricity Act 1989 in England and Wales, requiring regional electricity companies to provide a set amount of electricity from sources other than fossil fuel. The Scottish Renewables Order was brought into effect in late 1993. Accepted schemes will receive a premium price for electricity generated until 31 December 1998. Those schemes currently accepted under the 1990 and 1991 Renewables Order Tranches (i.e. requirements to provide renewable energy) include municipal solid waste (MSW), combustion (14 schemes providing 34 MW), scrap tyres (two schemes providing 84 MW) and landfill gas utilization (53 schemes providing 84 MW). The existing tranches cease in 1998. At the time of writing, announcement of schemes where applications have been successful under the third Renewables Order is awaited. The premium for this tranche is expected to apply for twelve years from the date of gaining planning permission for an accepted scheme rather than from the date of acceptance — as for former tranches — where this date may precede planning permission by many months or even years. This will enhance the value of the tranche as favourable terms will extend further into the operational phase of the schemes.

TREATMENT OF BULK SOLID WASTES

Incineration

This is the most effective method of reducing the volume of waste, as only 30–40 per cent by weight of the feed material remains for disposal. It is also the most costly and its popularity appears to be cyclic. In the 1930s, it was a popular method for the treatment of municipal wastes and became so again in the 1960s and early 1970s. However, with up to 30 per cent down-time, it became an extremely expensive process, the popularity declined and no new household waste incinerators have been commissioned in the UK in the past 15 years. Now, however, down-time of the plant has significantly reduced to a level of 15 per cent or less for municipal waste incinerators. With a decreasing supply of suitable waste disposal sites (particularly in the South East) and the increasing cost of land disposal, it is again becoming a viable method. Two major factors which affect the viability are: (1) the availability of high calorific value wastes (e.g. paper and plastics), which are reducing as a result of the government's recycling policy, and (2) the availability of government grants (the Non-Fossil Fuel Obligation), to foster the use of renewable energy sources.

Incineration is regarded as a suitable treatment method for household and commercial wastes and also for hazardous wastes. Although both types of waste require combustion at high temperatures in the presence of oxygen, the actual parameters are somewhat different. Household and commercial wastes require a residence period of two seconds at a temperature of 850°C, although this may be inadequate for particularly dense matter, e.g. logs, etc. Hazardous wastes require a residence period of two seconds at 1100°C or two seconds at 1200°C in the case of PCBs or other chlorinated materials.

31

Shredding/Pulverization

The two other main treatment methods which are available to reduce volume are shredding/pulverization and baling. However, both are expensive when used as a bulk reducing pre-treatment method for landfill. A similar reduction in volume can be achieved on the landfill site by competent operators with the proper site machinery.

Volume reduction by shredding/pulverization may be achieved by either a dry or wet process. The dry process is known as shredding and is carried out by a flail or hammer mill, generally having a vertical shaft, although plant is also available with a horizontal shaft. The flail or hammer smashes the waste, reducing it in size, after which the components can be separated ballistically or by air classification.The wet process is known as pulverization, and all such processes in this country are based on the Dano process. This is a horizontal rotating drum into which crude waste and a lubricant (usually water) are fed at one end and the treated waste, separated by size (usually a 34–45mm diameter screen), emerges from the other end. The smaller material (known as the fines or the product) is generally organic in nature, and the larger material (known as the rejects or contraries) is generally inorganic (glass, tin, etc.). A typical flow diagram for a pulverization process is shown in Figure 3.
These two processes are popular (in principle) as a treatment method, since not only do they reduce the bulk volume of wastes for transportation but to a certain extent they separate out the organic and inorganic fractions. The organic part of the waste can then be made into compost or refuse-derived fuel, and the inorganic constituents can be further separated out (or classified) for resource recovery. Items such as paper and rag cannot be recovered in this way, and are generally hand-picked prior to the treatment process. However, although these processes may be popular in principle, they have been used with limited success in the UK, mainly because of their cost and the difficulty of finding an end-use for the treated or recovered materials.

Another method of treating wastes to reduce volume is by baling. This is extensively used in Scotland, and involves the use of three hydraulic rams compressing the waste into bales which are about 1 tonne in weight and 1 m³ in volume. High pressure bales are self-sustaining. A certain amount of spring-back occurs when the pressure is released, but this nearly always happens in the first 48 hours and does not affect the overall stability of the bales. Most bales which are produced in this country are of medium pressure and are not self-sustaining, requiring banding to retain their shape.

Composting

This process is not popular in the UK but is used extensively in European countries, such as Holland and Germany, and in countries with hot climates. The composting process requires a warm climate to be efficient and results in a material which may be

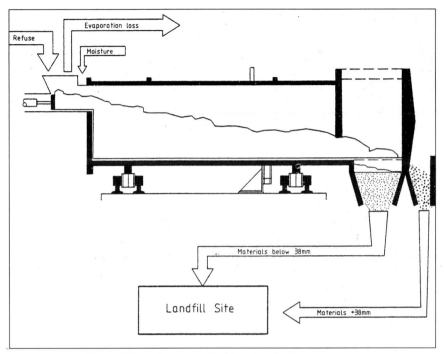

Within the figure:
Evaporation loss
Refuse
Moisture
Materials below 38mm
Landfill Site
Materials +38mm

Fig. 3 Flow diagram of wet pulverization process

high in metal content. Compost which is made from refuse alone can be deficient in nitrogen, although this imbalance is easily redressed by the addition of sewage sludge. It is generally used as a soil conditioner rather than a fertilizer and can improve the drainage of heavy soils and improve water retention in light sandy soils.

The composting process is aerobic, i.e. achieved through biological breakdown in the presence of oxygen, and therefore achieves fairly high temperatures (45–65°C) which, if maintained for 24 hours, are sufficient to ensure the elimination of a large number of pathogenic organisms.

Typically the waste (after pulverization, in this country) is 'windrowed', i.e. placed in long heaps up to 3m high, and regularly turned for about ten days to ensure the re-introduction of oxygen. After about three months of maturing in the windrow the material will have degraded to a stable humus-like substance which can then be screened to remove large inorganic objects and finally put to use.

Various attempts have been made to compost wastes in this country, usually after pulverization in the Dano process, but none has proved to be commercially viable in the long term.

Anaerobic Digestion

Anaerobic digestion is an increasingly popular concept for the treatment of wastes, although relatively few units are yet in operation (in the UK). The waste, with added liquids, is placed in purpose built containers and stirred to encourage mesophilic digestion. In principle, the same method is used for sludge digestion, but with 25–30 per cent solids, the end products comprise methane gas, a digested solid (which can be used like compost) and a liquid (requiring disposal). Materials such as plastic and wood, which float on top of the mixture, may be skimmed off and used, with the methane gas, to fuel the heating boiler. Operating as a continuous process, each container typically treats in the order of 100 000 tonnes per annum of household, commercial and some industrial wastes. Pretreatment comprises removal of metals and large items (e.g. concrete).

TREATMENT OF LIQUID WASTES

The majority of liquid (or slurry) wastes are hazardous and/or toxic, and generally fall into the 'difficult to handle' category. The treatment of liquid wastes is therefore carried out principally to make them acceptable for conventional disposal. This results in a reduction in their toxic effect and, generally, in their transformation into slurry or cake, which is transferred for instance to a landfill site, and a non-toxic liquid effluent which can be discharged to sewer. The treatment of leachate is described in Chapter 4.

The treatment of liquid wastes may be carried out by three basic methods: biological, physical and chemical.

Biological Treatment

This process is applicable to large volumes of waste whose toxic content is low, or from which the toxic element can easily be removed. The method relies upon bacteria and other biological organisms removing principally the organic pollutants from an aqueous waste stream and using their metabolism to change the pollutants to innocuous end-products. Treatment processes are similar to those which are employed for sewage treatment: preliminary settlement of insoluble solids, use of biological media to digest (aerobically or anaerobically) the organic content of the waste, final settlement and reduction of water content of the settled solids.

Depending upon the efficiency of the biological process, the aqueous effluent can be discharged directly to sewer, although it may require 'polishing' by chemical treatment. The sludge can be disposed of by soil injection, landfill, incineration or dumping at sea.

If a waste stream is amenable to biological treatment and there is sufficient capacity at the local sewage treatment works, the water utility may permit direct discharge of the entire waste stream to sewer. Whether the entire waste stream or the treated effluent is discharged, a licence to discharge will be required. This licence will set limits on volume and the concentrations of certain contaminants.

It should be noted that biological treatment methods are not amenable to shock loadings of contaminants; therefore the waste stream requires careful monitoring to safeguard against such an event.

Physical Treatment

Physical treatment is directed towards the separation of the solid and liquid phases. This includes such processes as screening and filter pressing, and may apply to the raw or treated waste stream. For the purposes of this booklet, solidification or encapsulation is considered with stabilization as chemical treatment.

Chemical Treatment

Although there are many forms of chemical treatment, they are all directed towards reducing the harmful effect of the waste. The principal methods are neutralization, thermal destruction and stabilization.

(i) *Neutralization*. Both acid and alkali streams can be neutralized, sometimes by mixing them together. As acidic effluents generally result from metal-plating processes, they contain metals in solution. On neutralization, the metal hydroxides are precipitated out of solution and can then be coagulated and separated from the aqueous liquor.

Cyanide wastes are treated by oxidation which transforms the cyanide into an innocuous form. Oxidation is carried out by the addition of an oxidizing agent such as ozone. However, further treatment of cyanide wastes is generally required as they usually contain heavy metals which are often complexed with the cyanide.

(ii) *Thermal Destruction*. Incineration is commonly used for the treatment/ destruction of hazardous wastes, both at the site of production (i.e. the factory) and commercially on a national scale.

Wastes, or effluents, having an organic content can readily be incinerated, as the organic fraction may allow autogenous burning, although some supplementary fuel may be required at start-up and to burn the inert residues. Liquid toxic wastes are more easily incinerated than solid toxic wastes, the latter being mainly drummed resins and contaminated dusts and soils.

There are estimated to be some 63 such incinerators in the UK operated by waste producers, dedicated to the disposal of their own hazardous wastes, including organic process liquors, solvents and distillation residues. Four plants are available on a commercial basis: the Rechem Environmental Service Ltd plants at Pontypool and Fawley (for liquids, sludges and solids); the Cleanaway Ltd plant at Ellesmere Port (for liquids, sludges and solids since 1990); and, the Leigh Environmental Ltd plant at Killamarsh, Derbyshire (liquids only).

The other basic division in type of waste for incineration (other than solid or liquid) is whether it is chlorinated or non-chlorinated. When burned, chlorinated wastes produce hydrogen chloride gas which attacks linings within the combustion plant and combines with water in the atmosphere to form hydrochloric acid. The requirement to remove this gas, generally by passing through water scrubbers, makes incinerators burning chlorinated wastes more complicated than those taking only non-chlorinated wastes. There is a further complication in that the waste from the water scrubber is then a contaminated effluent, and should be treated as such, and may not always be discharged direct to a sewer.

Polychlorinated biphenyl (PCB) wastes may only be disposed of by incineration in the UK. Partial combustion, i.e. oxidization, of these wastes results in the formation of dioxins and dibenzofurans, both of which are extremely toxic substances. For this reason, PCB wastes may only be burned in special incinerators where the temperature is maintained at 1200°C with a residence period of two seconds, with two per cent excess oxygen. The only plants in the UK which are suitable for burning PCB wastes are the Rechem plant at Pontypool and the Cleanaway plant at Ellesmere Port.

Clinical wastes have historically been disposed of by incineration at plant located on hospital sites. It is estimated that there are 900 such plants in the UK, generally operating on a batch basis, with less than 350 kg/hr rated throughput. With the removal of Crown Immunity in April 1991 and the new regulations for the control of emissions from small incinerators, it is anticipated that these incinerators will have to be replaced during the next few years to meet the higher standards.

Whilst incineration is the process of thermal destruction in the presence of oxygen, there is another process called 'pyrolysis' which is carried out in the absence of oxygen. Pyrolysis is only suitable for organic wastes but results in fuel by-products (a gas, an oil and a tarry residue) which can then be used as a supplementary fuel in another process. It is not used at present in the UK for hazardous waste treatment.

Incineration of hazardous wastes at sea was only permitted until 1994. As the plant used at sea was less sophisticated than on land, there was some restriction on the type of wastes for which this form of treatment was permitted. PCBs and other chlorinated wastes were not burned at sea.

(iii) *Stabilization.* This classification covers the processes of stabilization, solidification and encapsulation. Although they are different processes, they all result in a slurried cement mix containing hazardous waste which is designed to harden and contain the toxic elements of the waste. Strictly, the stabilization process involves the chemical bonding of the toxic elements, such as heavy metals, i.e. they cannot be leached out, for instance, by rainfall passing through the matrix. Encapsulation and solidification involve the physical trapping of the waste which means that, as the hardened solid breaks down, the toxic elements can be released into the leachate.

Two cement-mix processes have been operated in the UK with varying degrees of success. One process, the Sealosafe process, has been marketed in the UK under the trade name Stablex, and the other process was known as the Chemfix process. Both names imply that treatment is achieved by chemical bonding within the hydrated cement matrix. Whilst this is true for some pollutants, it is not true for all the waste streams for which the processes have been used. The Stablex process has been operated, under licence, by Cory Waste Management in Essex and by Leigh Interests in the Midlands. It is understood that the Stablex name has now been dropped although a chemical fixation process is still used by these operators. The Chemfix process was formerly operated under licence by Wimpey Laboratories, and is not used at present in the UK.

The process of hardening or solidification is achieved by various chemical additions to the base cement-waste mix. The exact proportions and identity of the added chemicals will depend on the waste stream to be treated. The basic Chemfix mix consisted of cement, waste and sodium silicate. The basic Sealosafe mix consists of cement, pulverized fuel ash (PFA) and a pre-treated, alkaline waste. Cory uses the process as a partial treatment prior to co-disposal of the slurry in household waste. The household waste therefore provides an attenuation zone for any substances which are leached out of the mix.

Leigh Interests have used the Sealosafe process as a treatment for toxic wastes prior to discharging them down a mineshaft. As with the Cory application, this proved to be acceptable only because any leachates were contained within the mine system.

These processes have occasionally failed in the past and are, as used at present, unsuitable for the treatment of organic wastes, but they have commercial potential. Research has been carried out at Imperial College, London and at Harwell into the mechanisms of encapsulation and stabilization, and into ways in which the processes can be improved to treat a wider range of wastes.

Treatment of Sewage Sludge

The volume of sewage sludge requiring land-based treatment is increasing due to the UK's response to the Urban Waste Water Treatment Directive, which requires treatment of sewage where none was previously provided, most notably at coastal locations, and the phasing out of sea disposal. It is estimated that the volume of sewage sludge requiring disposal will double by 1998, as a direct result of the Urban Waste Water Treatment Directive. Disposal to agricultural land has limited application and there is currently considerable interest in alternative methods of treating or utilizing the sludge. Whilst some water utilities have seriously examined recycling and utilization (for instance, Anglian Water Plc run a sludge composting plant), most favour incineration as the most viable option. There has, however, been considerable difficulty in promoting this option and although Yorkshire Water Plc have been successful in gaining permission for the development of a number of sludge incinerators, no other water company has been successful in this respect at the time of writing. However both Thames Water Plc and Wessex Water Plc are progressing towards planning applications for such plant.

The principal methods employed for the treatment of sewage sludge are (1) reduction of water content and (2) incineration.

(1) *Reduction of Water Content.* Sewage sludge is normally treated to reduce its water content by a combination of 'thickening' and 'pressing', or 'filtering', prior to final disposal. Thickening may be carried out generally by gravity and sometimes following the addition of chemicals. The solids are then separated from the supernatant liquid using a batch process called 'filter pressing', i.e. by feeding the mixture into a plate press under hydraulic pressure, the water being forced through the fabric between the press plates. A filter cake containing 30–40 per cent solids can be achieved by this method.

An alternative to pressing is by continuous filtering, the most common method in use being belt or drum filters. Essentially, thickened sludge is drawn by vacuum against a filter, the water passing through, and the solids remaining on the filter. A filter cake of 18–25 per cent solids can be achieved.

(2) *Incineration.* Thermal destruction of sewage sludge by incineration is used as a treatment method for about four per cent of the UK arisings. Until recently it has been unpopular because the high costs of fuel have made it unattractive compared to other methods of sewage sludge treatment and disposal. An ash residue remains for disposal — normally to land.

Treatment of Agricultural Wastes

A fairly wide range of treatment is available for agricultural wastes: incineration, drying, mechanical separation and biological treatment.

Incineration is a costly method and, as such, is not very attractive at present. It is only suitable for wastes containing a relatively high concentration of total solids such as poultry and some cattle wastes. The incinerated residue may have some value as a fertilizer.

Mechanical separation refers to the separation of the liquid and solid components of the waste, and is generally carried out to facilitate spreading onto agricultural land. The methods employed are similar to those used for sewage sludge dewatering and include vibrating screens, rotary screen presses and belt presses.

Biological processes for the treatment of agricultural waste encompass both aerobic and anaerobic degradation. Aerobic methods include composting, oxidation ditches, lagoons, biological filters and various methods of aeration. Anaerobic methods include septic tanks, lagoons, filters and digestion.

TREATMENT OF RADIOACTIVE WASTES

The method of treatment which is employed for radioactive wastes depends upon the level of radioactivity and the ultimate disposal route. In 1982 the Nuclear Industry Radioactive Waste Executive (Nirex) was set up as a result of a government White Paper (Cmnd 8607). Its responsibility was to develop comprehensive plans for the safe disposal of low and intermediate-level radioactive wastes, and was funded jointly by the Central Electricity Generating Board, British Nuclear Fuels Plc, United Kingdom Atomic Energy Authority and the South of Scotland Electricity Board. The government has retained the right to appoint two directors to Nirex. In November 1985, Nirex became incorporated as a public company (United Kingdom Nirex Ltd), shares being held by the former funding bodies of Nirex, and with the same responsibilities for the safe disposal of low and intermediate-level radioactive wastes. British Nuclear Fuels also disposes of some low-level wastes independently at its own sites (Drigg and Dounreay).

The management of high-level radioactive wastes is the responsibility of the United Kingdom Atomic Energy Authority and British Nuclear Fuels Limited.

Low-Level Wastes

Low level wastes are quantitatively defined as wastes with an activity greater than very low level wastes (i.e. greater than 400 kBq β+γ and volume less than 0.1 m³; or less than 40GBq β +γ for single items) but less than 40Bq/tonne α and less than 12GBq/t β+γ.

Low-level wastes comprise operational wastes such as paper, plastics, metal or glass with a trace contamination of radioactivity arising from nuclear facilities and from industrial and medical uses. Some wastes arising from the decommissioning of nuclear, industrial and medical radioactive plants are also classed as low-level waste because of the low level of radioactivity. Less than 30 per cent of low-level wastes arise from decommissioning activities.

Low-level wastes require no shielding during transportation and disposal, and Nirex have developed a range of containers which are suitable for their handling and transportation: 200-litre drums, a 3m³ box and 12m³ box, the last of these for large items of decommissioning wastes. For transport the 200-litre drums (the 'normal' or most commonly-used containers) will be loaded into an International Standards Organization (ISO) type freight container. Prior to disposal the drums will be compacted, loaded into a standard box and the voids between them filled with concrete.

Intermediate-Level Wastes

Intermediate-level wastes comprise similar types of waste to those described for low-level wastes, but with higher radioactive contamination. They arise principally at nuclear sites. Although some heat may be generated, it is not to such an extent that it has to be taken into account in either its treatment or disposal.

Intermediate-level wastes require shielding, and Nirex have developed a range of containers which is suitable for their handling and transportation.

High-Level Wastes

High-level wastes are defined loosely (in the UK) as wastes in which the temperature may rise significantly as a result of decay. The current strategy in the UK for such wastes is that they should be vitrified, i.e. converted into glass blocks and stored in metal casings for at least 50 years prior to disposal.

TRANSPORTATION OF WASTES

Three main options are available in the UK for the transportation of wastes: road, rail and barge, and the relative uses of these methods are given in Table IV.

Table IV. Methods of transportation for municipal waste

	Per cent by weight
Road	94
Rail	4
Barge	2

Road Transport

The majority of wastes are transported by road, about 70 per cent being transported directly to the waste disposal site in the initial collection vehicle. This may be in municipal collection vehicles (containing mainly household waste), tipper lorries or skips (containing commercial and dry industrial wastes), or tankers (containing liquid wastes).

Of the wastes which pass through a transfer or treatment station the majority are again transported by road. However, in this case the waste will generally have been packed into larger containers, where possible increasing the bulk density, to economize on transportation costs. Special vehicles are available for the bulk transportation of large volumes of waste.

Road transport is the most commonly-used method because waste tends to arise from discrete communities and may then be sent to disparate treatment or disposal sites, depending on its character and the capacity of the facilities which are available. It is common for a waste disposal authority to transport municipal waste from different parts of the town to different landfill sites, and for industrial and commercial wastes to be taken to different sites. Alternatively, municipal or industrial wastes may undergo a treatment process prior to final disposal.

Rail Transport

Rail transport may be used when (a) there is a good rail link between the waste source and the disposal or treatment site, and (b) large quantities of waste are generated at one place and the treatment or disposal site has capacity for this volume. It is not generally economic to transport less than 720 tonnes per train load. At an average capacity of 12 tonnes per ISO container this amounts to about 60 containers at one time. Municipal waste in the UK is generated at an average rate of a third of a tonne per person per year. Therefore, to fill a train load every week a minimum population of 112 000 is required to provide sufficient waste, together with a rail-linked transfer station.

Several large urban conurbations now use rail as a transportation method for their municipal waste, the most notable being Avonmouth, Manchester, Edinburgh and London. Generally, a loading terminal is built at the transfer station to which, if necessary, waste will be transported by road from other transfer stations. An unloading terminal must also be constructed at or near to the disposal site. As this is costly, it is generally only carried out at large capacity landfill sites or where potential disposal sites are close together, making the final road transfer feasible and economical. A former minerals loading rail facility may be in a suitable location to be refurbished for this use.

Barge Transport

Barge transport of waste has similar requirements to rail transport to make it economical: a large volume at one source, a large capacity site, and a water link. Because of this last requirement it is of far more limited application than rail transport, and has only been used successfully to transport London's waste to the Essex marshes disposal sites. As for rail transfer, the waste is loaded into ISO containers. It is then lifted onto and off the barges by special crane facilities constructed on the docks. At the landfill site the containers have to be transported by special lorries to the disposal point. The practice of loading the wastes directly onto open barges for subsequent unloading by grab crane at the disposal site has virtually ceased. It was felt to be most unsanitary, the waste being available to vermin and also open to rainfall, making it more difficult to handle on unloading.

6. DISPOSAL

INTRODUCTION

In this booklet the term 'disposal' is taken to mean the final resting place, and as such there are only two options, i.e. to land or to sea. The majority (as much as 97 per cent) of all wastes which are generated in the UK are disposed of ultimately to landfill, the remainder being dumped at sea. From 1998 all waste disposal will be land based.

The storage of wastes underground, e.g. in mine shafts and caverns, is considered separately from landfill as it is not generally accepted as a final disposal method. However, it is convenient to discuss it in this Chapter. Incineration of wastes does not usually result in total destruction, the residue requiring disposal in a landfill, and is therefore considered in Chapter 5.

LANDFILL

The landfill disposal of wastes has become a science, developed from the system of controlled tipping used in the UK since the 1930s. In the USA the method is known as sanitary landfill. There are still some badly-operated sites, and many which have not been properly engineered; however, standards have improved enormously over the last few years and are continuing to improve. As a result, waste disposal is becoming much safer and more acceptable in terms of minimizing environmental damage and the risk to human health. The requirements of the Environmental Protection Act 1990 will, now that they are in force, further improve standards through the imposition of stricter requirements for licensing, the granting of licences only to 'fit and proper' persons and the requirement to show that the site is not potentially damaging to the environment or human health before the licence can be handed back. Fit and proper persons are defined as not having a conviction for a relevant offence, being technically competent to run the site and being able to show that financial provision has been made to properly discharge the obligations of the licence.

General guidelines for the safe disposal of wastes in a landfill site are given in the DoE's Waste Management Papers 4 (as republished 1988) and 26 (published 1987). At the time of writing, these Waste Management Papers are under revision to comply with the EP Act 1990 waste licensing regulations. However, the general guidelines can be summarized as follows:

(i)   The site should be geographically or geologically located such that polluted water from the area cannot contaminate potentially usable aquifers, or, otherwise, a low-permeability engineered liner should be provided;

(ii) Wastes should be placed in layers generally 1–2m deep and compacted;

(iii) Inert cover should be provided to the wastes on a daily basis;

(iv) Litter and pests should be controlled;

(v) The site should be covered and restored to a use which is compatible with its nominated land use and its surroundings; and

(vi) Provision should be made for the monitoring and, if necessary, control of landfill gas and for the collection and treatment of leachate prior to discharge to a sewer or natural watercourse.

Types of Sites

Landfill disposal of wastes has been used, as the name suggests, to fill natural or man-made depressions in the landscape and to reclaim marginal land. Landraising is a term generally applied to the extension of a landfill site above the original ground contours, to maximize void space and extend the life of the site. The term is also used to describe the disposal of waste directly onto natural ground resulting in a raised land form.

Typical sites for landfill are quarries resulting from mineral extraction, valleys and depressions and disused railway cuttings. Marginal marshland can be raised and reclaimed using waste as fill material. Land can even be reclaimed from the sea, although this is not common practice in the UK.

Two methods of 'best landfill practice' have previously been acceptable in the UK: one favoured the 'dilute and disperse' philosophy, the other 'concentrate and contain'. The terms related primarily to the attitude towards leachate — the polluted water coming out of the waste. The 'dilute and disperse' method applies only to sites in permeable strata. Reliance is placed on there being sufficient depth of suitable geological strata (known as the attenuation zone) between the base of the landfill and any potentially usable aquifer capable of absorbing the polluting nature of the leachate. This basic philosophy for landfill site design is no longer favoured in the UK, and can only be adopted in special cases where the geology is well documented and there is little likelihood of a pathway developing to a potentially usable aquifer, the site itself not lying over any such aquifer. A further area of concern arising out of the use of these sites is that the geology is also permeable to landfill gas migration, the hazards of which are outlined later.

The 'concentrate and contain' philosophy assumes that no water within the site will be allowed to leave the area through the ground, either below or surrounding it. This gives maximum protection to all groundwater in the area and is the favoured practice in the UK. Leachate is collected within the site and is pumped out for treatment and discharge. Landfill gas may be effectively dealt with in a similar manner. If the geology is not such as to provide a sealed site, this must be provided by the preparatory engineering works.

Planning

Planning of a landfill site begins long before a planning application is lodged with the appropriate planning authority, i.e. county in England, district in Scotland and Wales and central government in Northern Ireland (see Chapter 3).

Whether it is a LAWDC or a private contractor who is seeking a disposal site, the planning and feasibility stages will be similar. The first task is to identify a suitable site to which waste can reasonably be transported by road, rail or barge. In parallel with this, the potential source(s) of waste must be identified in terms of type, volume and rate of waste generated, methods of transport available and pretreatment, if any is carried out.

It will then be necessary to examine the site to assess its suitability in terms of geology, volume, proximity to a suitable watercourse (preferably a sewer) for discharge of treated leachate and proximity to a suitable transport terminal. The preliminary financial viability of the operation will also be assessed. Discussion with the National Rivers Authority (NRA) usually takes place at this stage to ascertain whether or not a sensitive aquifer lies beneath or near the potential site.

If this preliminary screening process shows that a particular site may be appropriate for the disposal of an identified waste stream, the planning authority may be approached, on an informal basis, for their first views on the proposal. This allows the proposer to take account of any objections the planning authority may have before expensive site investigations and preliminary engineering design are carried out.

Guidelines for the site investigation are given in detail in Waste Management Papers 26 and 27. Waste Management Paper 26 (1986 version) gives guidelines for a 'detailed site investigation'. In summary, this includes geological and hydrogeological investigations and a topographical survey of the site. The site investigation report should identify features and give sufficient information for the following to be evaluated: site preparation work, water pollution prevention measures, pollution monitoring, landfill gas venting and control requirements, intermediate cover requirements, quantities of topsoil, subsoil and soil-making material available on site, estimated quantities of soil needed (to be imported for restoration) and vehicle and machinery requirements.

Waste Management Paper 27 (Landfill Gas) includes a survey of all man-made services and natural (i.e. geological) discontinuities around the site for a distance of 250m or further if features may present gas migration pathways outside this zone. This survey is intended to locate all (or as many as possible) of the potential gas migration pathways around the site. The remedial measures and preparatory works which are identified as necessary from this site investigation allow a more realistic assessment to be made of the costs of the proposed landfill operation.

Planning applications are supported by the results of the site investigations, together with an assessment of the possible impacts on the environment, amenity and where relevant, agriculture. An accompanying statement and drawings should also demonstrate preparatory engineering works and the method by which the disposal operation will be carried out, together with details of the final restoration of the site. It is generally advised to submit an Environmental Statement with a planning application for a landfill site. Neighbouring landowners must be notified of the application by notices posted on the site and in local newspapers, with the full application being available for view in a public place (school, library) local to the site.

Engineering Design

Engineering design of a landfill site encompasses all the preparatory works which are required to make the site suitable and safe for the disposal of the designated wastes, the necessary accompanying works, the detailed considerations of the phasing of the waste disposal operation, and the final restoration of the site.

Preparation works will include the design of such items as the engineered containment lining system, a leachate-collection system, cell construction, haul-road construction, provision and suitable location for storage of daily cover material.

Requirements to limit the polluting potential of landfill sites, arising out of the EC Groundwater Directive and the National River Authority's recently (1992) published Groundwater Protection Policy, have led to considerable development in liner technology in recent years. Site liners may be formed out of natural materials, such as clay which is engineered to a specified permeability limit, or low-permeability synthetic materials. Waste Management Paper 26 and the report of the North West Waste Disposal Officer's working group on liners (published 1988) provide guidance on the variety of liner methods available. Although some favour a composite liner design with an integral leak detection layer, the current trend is towards a flexible membrane in intimate contact with a clay layer. This is thought to provide the greatest degree of long term security, as the clay will provide containment for any local failure in the membrane. The provision of a leak detection layer permits the migration of contaminants to the point of weakness in the lower layer and is therefore thought to be less secure. The security of the liner system is entirely dependent on the quality of the preparation works, the quality of material storage and installation procedures and the degree of protection from damaging operational activities. This has led to the development of an auditing procedure known as CQA (construction quality assurance) to ensure that the security of the liner meets the design specification.

Other works on the site include the construction of a site access road, site fencing and notice boards, provision of a wheel cleaning facility, a weighbridge, site offices and a laboratory (required where hazardous or special wastes will be coming onto the site).

Phasing of the waste disposal operation will have to take account of the rate of waste input to the site, the overall water balance and the practical size for cell construction. The ideal situation is generally to minimize water ingress to the waste (and thereby leachate production) by keeping to a minimum the surface area of waste which is exposed to rainfall.

Engineering design of the restoration phase includes consideration of the final contours to encourage surface-water runoff, provision of a surface runoff collection system, inclusion of adequate capping material (such as clay), subsoil and topsoil for the proposed end use, and a planting scheme for the final restored surface. Filling to achieve the proposed contours must take into account settlement of the waste due to compaction and decomposition, and the differential effect of waste settling against the boundary of the site and at the cell walls.

Sundry other works include the provision of sight and noise barriers to protect local residents from disturbance during the operation, and the provision of a landfill gas monitoring and collection system. Gas monitoring (see Waste Management Paper 27) is generally carried out from boreholes. This may require the construction of an inert layer around the waste, within the site, if access cannot be gained to land outside the site to place boreholes. The permission of the relevant landowner and the planning authority is required for the drilling of boreholes.

Leachate

Leachate is water which has come into contact with degrading refuse and contains contaminants from that refuse in suspension or solution. Sources of this water are rainfall, groundwater infiltration, water contained within the refuse itself (typically 20–25 per cent in domestic refuse), water from liquid waste disposal and water resulting from the biological decomposition of organic wastes (Figure 4).

Contaminants which are present in leachate are typically metals, organic acids and esters, ammonia and other nitrogenous compounds. Pesticides and PCBs may also be present, although this is very rare. Leachate generally has a high chemical oxygen demand and low oxygen content although, as with all the parameters mentioned here, these will vary widely from site to site and with the age of waste within the site. Under the Controlled Waste Regulations 1992 (SI, 1992 No. 588) leachate from a deposit of waste is to be treated as trade effluent and, therefore, comes under all the controls and licensing requirements for that type of waste.

On a 'dilute and disperse' site, the leachate is allowed to percolate out of the site into the rock below, relying on the physical entrapment of the solids and the chemical alteration of contaminants in solution to prevent serious groundwater pollution.

For a 'concentrate and contain' site it is necessary to collect the leachate for treatment prior to discharge away from the site to a suitable watercourse or sewer.

The general philosophy for leachate management in a contained site is to keep the head of leachate as low as possible or below the level of surrounding groundwater to minimize the pressure on the containment system and to ensure that clean water will flow into the site rather than dirty water out. Collection of the leachate can be undertaken from the base of the landfill with a herringbone-type structure of collection pipes; or, preferably, by the provision of a basal drainage layer across the whole site with sumps at the lowest point(s).

Discharge of leachate to a natural watercourse or a sewer requires a discharge consent under the Control of Pollution Act 1974 or the Water Resources Act 1991. If granted, a consent will set upper limits for certain contaminants anticipated to be present in the leachate, which may prove harmful to the watercourse. If a consent is granted for discharge to a sewer, the leachate will be treated as a trade effluent (or an industrial effluent if tankered to a sewage works). In this case, the water utility or regional council will make a charge for the discharge to cover the cost of treatment at its own works; the charge may be based on a formula which considers such aspects as volume, chemical oxygen demand, suspended solids and may also include multiples of the concentrations of other parameters.

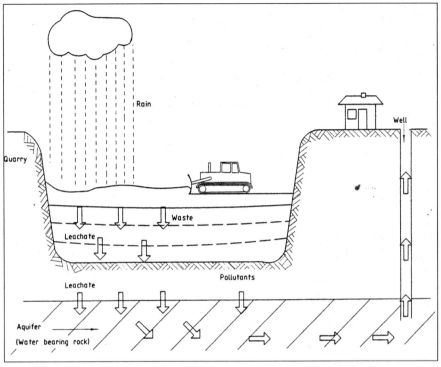

Fig. 4 Environmental impact: groundwater pollution

Whether the discharge is to a river or to a sewer, it is generally necessary to treat the leachate prior to discharge; firstly to achieve the consent limit and, secondly, to minimize the charge which is payable. As ammonia is the major contaminant in leachate and the potentially most harmful substance to a river (kills fish) or a sewer (harmful to biological treatment processes at sewage treatment works), most leachate treatment is aimed at reducing ammonia and the chemical oxygen demand. The most frequently-used treatment method is that of oxidation. This can be achieved by the addition of chemicals or by aeration. Combinations of the two methods have been used with varied success, as have biological methods such as activated sludge or biological filters or contactors. With biological methods, it is generally necessary to add nutrients such as phosphorus or phosphoric acid, to enable the biomass to thrive. Recirculation of leachate through the waste as a biological reactor is thought to reduce the strength of some leachates and can be achieved by spraying over the surface or by direct injection into the waste. A special licence may be required for this. Direct dilution with clean water is another possible method. With the current changes in legislation and attitudes towards environmental liability, it is becoming necessary to treat leachate to ever higher standards, particularly prior to discharge to natural water bodies. Sophisticated treatment and effluent polishing systems are therefore being applied to leachate and include the use of activated carbon, reverse osmosis and distillation.

As treatment of any form is an additional cost in the operation of the site, good practice now centres on reducing as far as possible the volume of leachate (and hence the volume to be treated). This requires operation of the site in such a manner that all clean (i.e. not been in contact with waste) rainfall runoff and groundwater seepages are collected separately from the leachate and that the surface of waste exposed to (and able to absorb) rainfall is kept to a minimum. Clean waters can be discharged with little (possibly settlement alone) or no treatment to a watercourse or allowed to soak away into the ground.

There is considerable debate at the time of writing as to the best way to manage leachate. The minimization of leachate production is generally favoured as the best environmental option for the currency of the landfill site. However, keeping the waste dry retards and prolongs both the degradation processes and the potential for harm to the environment and reduces the likelihood of a completion certificate being issued for the site.

Landfill Gas

Landfill gas typically comprises methane (60 per cent) and carbon dioxide (40 per cent), and is produced as a result of the decomposition of organic waste. Methane is flammable in air at a range of 5–15 per cent concentration by volume, provided that an ignition source and sufficient oxygen are present. Carbon dioxide has asphyxiating properties and is normally present in air at 0.03 per cent by volume. Guidelines in Waste Management Paper 27 give safe levels within a dwelling: less than 1 per cent for methane, and less than 1.5 per cent for carbon dioxide. Above these levels, action, such as active venting and/or evacuation, should be taken.

During recent years, landfill gas has become a matter of public concern because of a number of 'incidents' (explosions), the most serious of which occurred in Loscoe, Derbyshire in 1986. No one has yet been killed in the UK as a result of one of these explosions, but there have been injuries. There have also been a number of cases of asphyxiation from landfill gas. This has prompted the DoE to publish the guidelines in

Waste Management Paper 27 and to sponsor research to provide further knowledge of the production and migration mechanisms of landfill gas. Under the Environmental Protection Act 1990 there is provision (not yet in force at the time of writing) for the Secretary of State to issue regulations, directions and guidance analogous to the guidance previously provided by the series of Waste Management Papers. It is thought that regulations relating to landfill gas management may be among the first to be made and will be based on the guidance given in Waste Management Paper 27.

The problems relating to landfill gas have arisen from two main causes: the first is the way in which waste is landfilled, and the second is the increasing reuse of derelict land for redevelopment.

Placing well mixed, biodegradable waste in a sealed landfill site, adding an optimum amount of water, covering daily and finally placing a low permeability cover over it creates ideal conditions for the production of landfill gas (Figure 5). If no measures are taken to remove this gas by venting or flaring, pressure can build up to a level which encourages the gas to migrate along easy pathways such as natural rock fissures or man-made services. The same effect is achieved by changes in atmospheric pressure. The gas can thus make its way off-site (migration distances of up to 400m have been recorded) and into buildings where electric sparks and cigarettes can provide the ignition source required to cause an explosion.

The re-use of derelict land for redevelopment has led to considerable development on or near to previously closed landfill sites. These sites are unlikely to have had gas control measures installed, and development adjacent to such a site should be treated with caution. The Interdepartmental Committee for the Redevelopment of Contaminated Land (within the DoE) issue guidelines for the type of site investigation which should be carried out prior to the development of any derelict land site and guidance on the development of land next to landfill sites. This includes a survey to establish whether methane gas is present on the site — and whether the gas is residual, being generated, or migrating on to the site.

Most planning authorities now require consideration to be given to the monitoring and control of landfill gas at the planning application stage. Although it is not strictly a planning or land-use issue, it does affect the potential use of that land or of adjacent land. There will almost certainly be site licence conditions imposed requiring landfill gas to be monitored, and controlled if necessary.

Guidelines are given in Waste Management Paper 27 for both the monitoring and control of landfill gas. Its commercial use is considered in Waste Management Paper 26.

51

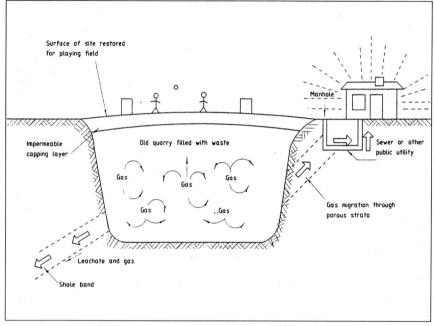

Fig. 5 Environmental impact: landfill gas

In summary, monitoring should take place at the edge of the landfill site, at a point approximately half way between the edge of the fill material and the nearest property at risk, and adjacent to the property. If no such property exists within 500m of the site, then monitoring should be carried out at 250m and 500m from the fill materials. Although not precisely stipulated, it is generally accepted that monitoring points should be boreholes sunk to the approximate depth of the landfill.

Control measures will depend upon the particular geology surrounding the site and the proximity of local development (present and proposed). A low permeability barrier may be required to prevent gas migration off-site. Adjacent to this should be placed a venting ditch, for example, filled with stone to give a large void ratio. It may be sufficient to allow this ditch to vent direct to atmosphere, in which case measures must be taken to prevent soil and plants sealing the surface. If, however, this is insufficient, a gas collection system may be installed. This may be placed as part of the venting ditch, or as a herring-bone lateral and chimney system, or a combination of both. Design of these systems should take into consideration the final restoration and proposed end use of the site; for example, ploughing activities should not be capable of ripping up the gas collecting system.

Landfill gas may be used as a source of fuel. The hindrance to its use is generally the difficulty of finding a potential user within economic distance of the site. However, there are now many instances in the UK where landfill gas is used commercially, and several where it has been converted to electricity (see Chapter 5). The Renewables Orders under the NFFO should encourage the further use of landfill gas.

Reinstatement

Landfill sites can be restored to suit three types of end use: (a) amenity or recreation, (b) agriculture, and (c) 'hard' development (building), and this should be taken into consideration at the planning stage. Generally in the UK, hard development is not encouraged as a proposed end use for a potential landfill site, although it is being increasingly considered for very old landfill sites (see previous section).

Amenity is the most common form of after-use, the area being landscaped for walking or for wildlife. Differential settlement is then not a significant problem but the capping must be sufficient to support suitable planting regimes (e.g. bushes and trees) and, in some cases, ponds and surface water courses. Recreational use is a favourable after-use in an urban or semi-urban area. This use requires the site to be filled so that the final settlement is fairly even to prevent, for example, ponding occurring on a sports field. However, it does not require a great depth of sub and topsoil over the capping layer, as the principal vegetation is grass.

Agricultural after-use is preferred in rural areas, although with a surplus of good agricultural land at the time of writing, it is likely that restored landfills in agricultural areas will be incorporated into 'set-aside' schemes, i.e. likely to remain fallow. However, the standard of restoration must be suitable for later agricultural use. Landfilling has previously frequently occurred through the infill of valleys leased from a farmer who required them to be returned for his use on completion. In this case, a small amount of differential settlement would not be quite as important as for a sports field, provided that there is adequate drainage. However, a good depth of sub and topsoil is required to prevent the capping layer from being ploughed up and damaged. Also, an increased depth will be required where trees or hedges are to be planted.

Waste Management Paper 26 gives guidelines for the depth of capping layer, and sub and topsoils required. These should be treated as minimum depths, and discussions should be held with the planning authority as to their general requirements.

General practice is to place a low permeability layer, such as clay, over the landfill site prior to the placing of sub or topsoil. A suitable thickness is considered to be 0.75-1.00m, to prevent ingress of rain-water to the site. However, clay will crack if it is allowed to dry out, permitting both water ingress and gas egress. Evidence of the cracks is usually given by vegetation die-back where the accumulation of gas has starved roots of oxygen, killing the plants.

Various alternatives to this practice have been tried, and research is currently being carried out to monitor the efficacy of some of these alternatives. Some possibilities include: (a) the use of a permeable layer (to collect the gas) below the clay layer, (b) a combination of natural materials to provide a flexible low permeability layer which will not crack, or (c) the use of a combination of synthetic and natural materials (such as an impermeable synthetic layer or bentonite mat underlying a drainage layer).

Obviously, the design of the final capping layer and restoration surface will have to take account of such items as the gas control system, and the need to keep a venting ditch open to the atmosphere. If leachate recirculation by injection is being considered as a method of treatment, provision will have to be made for this below the capping layer.

Because the capping layer is generally of low permeability, the restoration contours have to be designed to encourage runoff. To prevent this runoff entering the waste at the edge of the site, it is usual to install some sort of collection system at the site perimeter. This should be kept totally separate from the leachate system, and may be discharged to a watercourse or into a soakaway system remote from the site.

Types of Wastes

The types of waste which may be placed in a landfill site are limited by the conditions of the site licence. Most waste regulation authorities have a range of categories of waste, and will normally limit a site licence to certain of these categories, with specified exclusions. A limit may also be placed on tonnages of specific wastes over certain time periods.

Typical categories of waste are:

(i) 'Inert' materials, generally including building materials but not asbestos;

(ii) Materials of 'low biodegradability' such as non-hazardous industrial wastes containing some organic matter, for example paper and plastic wastes, road gully washings;

(iii) 'Biodegradable' wastes including household waste;

(iv) 'Difficult' wastes, which are those requiring special handling but which are not necessarily toxic or hazardous; and

(v) 'Hazardous' wastes which include hazardous and special wastes, also asbestos.

The types of wastes allowed in a certain site will depend on the type of site, i.e. containment or dispersal, and on the sensitivity of the site in terms of local opposition or sites of special interest. For instance, unlined sites in chalk, overlying currently or potentially usable aquifers may only be permitted to take the inert category of waste. Alternatively a site in low permeability clay remote from any aquifer may be permitted to take difficult and hazardous wastes. The treatment of such wastes (see later) may make them more acceptable for disposal at a greater number of sites.

Most wastes which are disposed of in a landfill site are solid in nature. However, with careful attention to the overall water balance, sludges, silts and slurries may also be disposed of in this way. Liquid hazardous wastes may be placed in a landfill site by a method known as co-disposal.

Co-disposal
Co-disposal is a term which is used for the controlled disposal together of household wastes and a limited range of solid or liquid industrial wastes. The process takes advantage of beneficial interactions between the waste types such that there is no detectable impact on leachate quality.

Two techniques are employed for the actual placing of the waste. The first involves placing the two types of waste in alternate layers with daily cover on top of both. This method may be appropriate for silts and sludges, provided that it does not present handling difficulties.

The second method requires the prior disposal of solid, absorbent wastes, such as household waste, by the normal landfilling method — in layers with inert daily cover. Trenches are then dug into this material and the liquid, slurry or sludge is poured into these. The absorbent waste already in place soaks up the liquid and acts as an attenuation zone for gross contaminants if the liquid is hazardous or toxic.

Considerable research has been carried out, mainly by the Water Research Centre and Harwell, into the co-disposal of various combinations of waste. The results of this research provide the basis for the UK policy of promoting co-disposal.

Treatment Prior to Disposal
Chapter 5 considers all kinds of waste treatment from simple compaction in a transfer

station, through the various requirements to facilitate resource recovery, to the treatment of hazardous wastes. Incineration is also discussed.

Treatment of bulk (non-hazardous) wastes prior to landfill reduces the volume requiring disposal, and simple compaction at a transfer station can assist the achievement of good compaction ratios on the landfill site. Pulverization or shredding increases bulk density considerably and further aids final compaction; it also encourages rapid biodegradation with fairly even settlement. Since pulverization and shredding may be used as a first step in the process of resource recovery, the removal of such materials as can be reused will reduce the volume for both transportation and disposal. This should be taken into account when considering the relative costs of the treatment process compared to the costs for transportation and disposal. However, consideration should also be given to the fact that, with materials such as metals and glass recovered, the remaining wastes have a higher organic content than before. This may lead to the production of a higher strength leachate, depending on the composition of the feed stock.

Baling as a treatment process results in wastes which are easy to handle in transportation and on site. However, the compaction ratio which is achieved on site is not significantly different from that which is achieved through prior pulverization or by using good compaction equipment. Water is not easily able to percolate through the waste and biodegradation may, as a result, be inhibited.

Treatment by incineration leaves a residue (30–40 per cent by volume of the feed material) which should be biologically inert and is generally disposed of to landfill. This residue may be high in heavy metal content but, provided that this is acceptable at the disposal site, it may be used in place of or to supplement the inert daily cover material.

DISPOSAL AT SEA

Disposal at sea is reserved for wastes for which a suitable route does not exist on land. Therefore inert materials, demolition materials and domestic waste tend not to go by this route; whereas difficult and hazardous wastes, sewage sludge and, until recently, radioactive wastes were all disposed of at sea. This method of disposal has been considered in the UK to be the best practicable environmental option for certain wastes, particularly in view of our small land area and easy access to the sea. However, the UK has been under pressure from the other EC Member States and from the other members of the North Sea Commission to reduce this practice and consider ceasing it altogether. An agreement was signed in 1987 between the members of the North Sea conference to restrict dumping at sea by 1992 and to attempt to further reduce the quantities after this date. The dumping of liquid industrial wastes at sea stopped in 1992 and marine incineration ceased in 1994.

The disposal of waste at sea comes under the jurisdiction of the Ministry of Agriculture, Fisheries and Food (MAFF), who have an obligation to see that all land disposal options have been considered and found not to be feasible, before they will issue a licence for sea disposal.

Hazardous Wastes

Hazardous wastes were historically transported for both incineration at sea and deep sea dumping but these practices have now ceased.

Radioactive Wastes

Up to 1956 at least, Nirex considered marine disposal to be the best environmental option for low and intermediate-level radioactive wastes. A number of sites have been used by the UK, commencing in 1951. Most are to the west of Britain and the EC Member States, although the Hurd Deep in the English Channel was used during the 1950s and early 1960s, and a site north-west of Ireland was used occasionally in the early 1950s. The Holliday report, *Report of the Independent Review of Disposal of Radioactive Waste in the North-East Atlantic* (1984) fully describes the UK practice of annually dumping radioactive wastes at sea.

The dumping of solid radioactive waste in the North-East Atlantic was suspended in 1983 and is no longer considered to be an acceptable practice. Such wastes are stored at specified locations in the UK (such as Sellafield) until a suitable land-disposal route can be found for them. However, the practice of discharging liquid effluents contaminated with radioactivity is still carried out. The discharge outfall from the nuclear plant at Sellafield has been the subject of frequent attention from environmental pressure groups such as the media and Greenpeace.

Sewage Sludge

The disposal of sewage sludge to sea has historically been widely practised in the UK, with about 28 per cent going by this route in 1990. This proportion is changing due to the combined effects of the Urban Waste Water Treatment Directive (which will cause more sludge to be generated) and the 1987 North Sea Treaty (which requires the marine dumping of sewage sludge to be phased out by 1998).

There are eleven locations around the UK coast which have been licensed and used for the disposal of sewage sludge (Table V). All but the site on the Clyde are rapid dispersion sites, swept by tidal currents.

Table V. Sewage sludge dumping sites in UK

Firth of Forth (2 sites)	Plymouth
Tyne/Tees	Falmouth (now disused)
Humber	English Channel
Thames (3 sites)	Liverpool Bay
Isle of Wight	Firth of Clyde
Lyme Bay	

Sewage sludge is principally taken by barge to disposal sites licensed by MAFF, little being discharged by pipeline. It is not containerized and is disposed of by discharging from the bottom of the barge. The sludge may or may not be treated (to reduce the moisture content and hence increase the volume transported at one time) prior to filling the barge.

DISPOSAL UNDERGROUND

This disposal route is separate from the use of waste to infill quarries and other holes in the ground, and is applied to the deep disposal of wastes in mineshafts, worked-out mines or in specially engineered deep geological repositories. It is generally used as an intermediate storage option rather than ultimate disposal.

Deep underground disposal is normally reserved for the disposal or storage of hazardous or radioactive wastes. There are certain geological formations in the UK which are considered to be fairly secure in that they either have extremely low permeability or are known to be sealed from contact with any aquifers (for instance, the deep mine shafts at Brownhills in the Midlands, used by Leigh Interests). The intention is that highly dangerous wastes should be securely contained where they can easily be monitored and retrieved if necessary, until by-products can be recovered or a safe disposal route can be found. This is a particularly useful method for wastes which decay and generate heat, such as radioactive wastes.

Radioactive Wastes Underground

UK Nirex Ltd is responsible for managing the safe disposal of low and intermediate-level radioactive wastes.

A programme to investigate and provide further near-surface repositories was carried out between 1985 and 1987. The findings of this programme have led Nirex to conclude that 'The economic advantages of near-surface low-level waste disposal were not as great as had been considered earlier. Although near-surface disposal of low-level waste would be safe, the development of a new near-surface repository for low-level waste showed no significant cost advantage when compared with the marginal cost of disposing of low-level waste along with intermediate-level waste in a deep repository, even allowing for the cost of any storage of low-level waste needed before disposal' (Nirex Annual Report 1987–88).

Shallow burial of wastes was abandoned in 1987. An extensive site selection programme has now confirmed that deep (about 900m) disposal below Sellafield is the preferred option.

High-level radioactive wastes, when generated, will be encased in glass (vitrified) and stored in layers in the Sellafield repository where they can be monitored remotely.

MISCELLANEOUS WASTES/ROUTES

Agricultural Wastes

The principal route for the disposal of agricultural wastes is land disposal. The principal waste stream is manures and bed litter which may be a liquid, slurry or wet solid and hence sprayed, injected or spread and ploughed in as appropriate. A small per centage (e.g. of poultry waste) is recycled through use in the production of feedstock or of energy under the NFFO. At the time of writing, a ruling is awaited on whether agricultural wastes are to be classified as Controlled Wastes; they currently are not categorized as such. Chemical wastes (including pesticides, herbicides and fertilizers) generated by farming activities are not currently subject to any disposal controls provided they are disposed of on the farmer's own lands; however, if disposed of off this land, they become subject to the regulations governing controlled waste.

Sewage Sludge

Whilst about 13 per cent of sewage sludge is disposed of to landfill, about 46 per cent is disposed of to farmland (1990 figures). It is normal to thicken or dewater sewage sludge which is destined for disposal at a landfill site but, even so, it is difficult to handle in this environment. Disposal to agricultural land does not require prior treatment of the sludge, but is subject to strict controls regarding gross loading of pollutants such as heavy metals.An EC Directive was implemented in June 1989 which limits the application of sewage sludge to agricultural land by stipulating either the gross loading in any one application or the period of time over which such loading may take place.

In the past, methods of application were restricted to spraying, which was cheap and easy. However, the objectionable odours which were released by this method have led to the development of more aesthetically acceptable techniques such as subsoil injection of the sludge. This may be carried out by dragging a spray nozzle in the ground on a line suspended behind a tractor or by driving a mole through the ground whilst injecting.

Increased volumes of sewage sludge requiring land-based disposal have persuaded the water utilities to examine carefully the options available to them and a number now favour incineration: Yorkshire Water Plc has led the field in this area.

7. ECONOMICS

The cost of waste disposal includes all activities from collection at the source through transfer, treatment and transportation to ultimate disposal, environmental monitoring and rectification. It therefore includes such items as vehicle and plant costs, maintenance, standing time, labour, fuel, landscaping, planting, monitoring, and discharge costs (i.e. for leachates and contaminated waters to sewer). It also includes payback for preparatory costs of design, the work required to obtain either planning permission or a licence and the care and maintenance of the site until the certificate of completion is granted.

Table VI shows typical costs and charges for different parts of this process, calculated for household (municipal) waste.

Waste disposal cost data have always been notoriously inaccurate, due largely to the lack of management data on which to base the calculations. Until fairly recently, most landfill sites accepted waste by the 'load' and operators and WRA officers used rules of thumb to translate this into volume or tonnages. Even with the majority of landfill sites now using weighbridges to determine the weight of waste coming into their sites, there is still considerable variability in the precise definition of various categories of waste and, therefore, variability in charges around the country. Other factors which affect cost are mainly commercial, such as parity with competitors, the necessity to have lined the site, the cost of environmental monitoring and the cost of implementing changes to the licence required in the transition from a COPA 74 licence to an EPA 90 licence. Provision will also now have to be made for funds to be set aside to remedy any environmental damage arising from activities at the site. With costs for the relocation of licensed abstraction wells currently cited at around £2.5 million, considerable sums may have to be set aside in this way. WRAs appear to favour the setting up of an escrow account for this purpose, with both licence holder and WRA as signatory, with regular payments into it arising from an increase in the disposal charge per tonne.

Since 1991, the government has been considering the use of economic instruments rather than regulation to achieve its environmental goals. The government wishes to promote recycling to achieve the stated aim for the UK of recycling 25 per cent of household waste by the year 2000. The introduction of waste recycling credits has not so far had sufficient influence on the way in which wastes are managed and, in 1993, Coopers and Lybrand published research into the use of economic instruments in the field of wastes management. Entitled *Landfill Charges and Prices: Correcting Possible Market Distortions,* the report explores the influence that a levy on landfill disposal would have on the management of wastes. The report concluded that a levy of at least £20 per tonne was required to have any significant effect and that, as a consequence, the proportion of household waste recycled would rise from 2 to 12 per cent; that incinerated would rise from 15 to 38 per cent. Thus, although waste disposal costs would rise very significantly, the target for the recycling of household wastes would not be met. At the time of writing the Treasury has just announced the introduction, in 1996, of a landfill tax. The level at which it may be set and the subsequent effect on wastes management practices have yet to be determined.

The Coopers & Lybrand report contains the most recent attempt to collect economic data on waste disposal and these figures form the basis of the data given in Table VI.

Table VI. Waste Management Costs

	£/tonne
Recycling	
Bring	16–36
Blue box	85–175
Green bin	55–70
Green bag	55–85
Composting	35–50
Incineration:	
Household wastes	15–25
Hazardous wastes[1]	
Landfill:	
Household wastes	5–25[2]
Commercial wastes	5–30[3]

Notes
(1) Costs vary widely, depending on whether co-disposed in landfill, incinerated or treated, e.g. by stabliization.
(2) Mainly £5–20/tonne
(3) Mainly £10–15/tonne

The wide range in the costs given in Table VI generally reflects the difference between scattered and concentrated communities and the effect of being unable to place, for example, a landfill site within an urban area. In Wales, rural areas have higher costs of disposal than urban areas; in England the reverse is true. This apparent paradox may be accounted for by the relatively high costs of small-scale operations in Wales and by the need for expensive treatment methods at the large urban conglomerations in England.

Depending on the type of waste and its amenability to treatment, costs can range from those shown in Table VI for landfill disposal to five hundred or even a thousand times those figures. For instance a one-tonne load of solid-state capacitors contaminated with PCBs could cost about £1300 to incinerate, plus the handling and transport charges involved in transferring it to the incinerator.

Table VII (overleaf) lists items which should be considered in arriving at costs for landfill.

Table VII. Activities to be conside

(a) Site Assessment	(b) Site Development	(c) Site Operation
Reconnaissance	Acquisition of site	Operatives — wages/salaries
Market survey	Detailed design	Plant — lease/repair/
Preliminary ground investigation	Surface water diversion/ re-routing	maintenance — fuel/oil
Full geological and hydrogeological investigation	Groundwater cut-off/ separation	Imported cover material Site maintenance
Outline landfill design	Lining — natural/artificial	Environmental
Planning and disposal licence consultations etc.	Leachate collection/ removal/treatment	— control, e.g. pests/litter — monitoring, e.g. water/gas
	Earthworks — topsoil strip/store	Surveying
	— bunds/embankments/roads — cover material stockpile	Leachate
	Other	— treatment/disposal charges
	— access roads	
	— screening/fencing/planting	Gas
	— office/laboratory	— venting/pumping
	— utilities	
	— wheel cleaner/weighbridge/ garages etc.	Rates
	Gas — monitoring installations — control — utilization	

(d) Site Restoration	(e) Site Aftercare (for up to 15 years)
Capping — clay — subsoil replacement — topsoil replacement — conditioning/nutrient addition	Maintenance and cultivation Differential settlement and treatment Leachate — treatment/disposal
Drainage — runoff	Gas — venting/utilization
Planting — grass — hedges/trees	Environmental monitoring — leachate/gas — groundwater
Cultivation and maintenance	

Plate 1.   Refuse collection vehicles *(Cleanaway Ltd.)*

Plate 2.   Paper for recycling *(Biffa Waste Services Ltd.)*

Plate 3.   Recycled green waste compost *(The Waste Company)*

Plate 4. High temperature incinerator at Ellesmere Port *(Cleanaway Ltd.)*

Plate 5. Compactor on landfill *(Biffa Waste Services Ltd.)*

Plate 6. Lining a landfill (*W. S. Atkins*)

71

Plate 7. Leachate Treatment works, Gairloch landfill site, Scotland
(Aspinwall & Company Ltd.)

Plate 8. Landfill gas monitoring *(Biffa Waste Services Ltd.)*

73

Plate 9.   Flaring excess gas from utilization scheme *(W. S. Atkins)*

74

GLOSSARY

There are many categories of waste, although for the purpose of this book they are broken down into three broad bands: non-hazardous, hazardous and radioactive. Agricultural wastes and sewage sludge are included here only as regards their ultimate disposal. The management of sewage sludge has been otherwise dealt with in a CIWEM booklet entitled *An Introduction to Sewage Treatment*.

Within the three broad bands defined above there is a further breakdown of types of waste, for instance for solid waste these include domestic, commercial and industrial. This further breakdown of the categories is given below, with each category briefly defined.

NON-HAZARDOUS WASTES

Controlled waste

This is a term defined by the Environmental Protection Act 1990 (see Chapter 2) and includes household, industrial and commercial waste.

Household waste

This is waste which is produced by private residential homes, by educational and nursing (including hospitals — but not clinical wastes) establishments. It comprises all waste produced as part of day-to-day living. A typical analysis is given in Table III.

Civic amenity waste

Civic amenity waste is the bulky waste taken by householders to civic amenity collection sites provided under the Refuse Disposal (Amenity) Act 1978.

Commercial waste

Waste from premises used wholly or mainly for the purpose of a trade or business or for the purpose of sport, recreation or entertainment.

Industrial waste

Waste from a factory or industrial premises. This category excludes mine and quarry wastes but includes construction waste, dredging spoil and sewage sludge (see below).

Trade effluent

Waste substances — usually liquid in nature — arising from a factory or industrial process. They may be hazardous or non-hazardous. (In the context of this book, only hazardous trade effluents are considered and, of these, only those which are not disposed of, without treatment, to sewer.) In recent years, there has been a general policy to recycle and recover as many as possible of the by-products of an industrial process. These trade effluents are, therefore, more similar to a sludge than a liquid, and are fairly toxic in nature.

Difficult wastes

A term used by local authorities for wastes which require special care in their handling, treatment or disposal. This is a wider category than hazardous waste and some, but not all, difficult wastes may be hazardous.

Putrescible wastes

This is a term applied to wastes which can very easily be broken down by biological action. Typical wastes which are putrescible are food and vegetable wastes in domestic waste, sewage sludge, agricultural manure wastes, wastes from food-processing factories, tanneries, glue factories. Wastes which have a high cellulose content such as rice and wheat husks, paper and wood, although they are biodegradable, are not generally considered to be putrescible. They are, however, capable of generating methane and other gases and carry a potential environmental liability.

Inert wastes

Inert wastes are those which are biologically and chemically stable. Depending on the precise definition used by the waste disposal authority, this category is generally taken to include building wastes and subsoils. However, contaminants can be leached out (chemical action) of the building wastes, and the organic matter in soil and subsoil can degrade (biological action).

Sewage sludge

Sewage sludge results from the treatment of sewage. The characteristics of the sludge will depend on the method of treatment employed. Sludge from primary settling tanks has less water than other sludges (92–97 per cent) but may contain high concentrations of metals and bacteria. Sludge from humus tanks or clarifiers is more flocculent, but may also be more filamentous in nature and difficult to dewater than primary sludge. It may have similar or lower heavy metal and bacteria concentrations. For this reason it is often co-settled with primary sludge. Any sludge treated in an anaerobic digester has a reduced organic content and is more pleasant to handle. It is difficult to dewater mechanically but dries easily on beds. Sludge which has been treated with coagulants has a significantly lower water content than other sludges.

Agricultural wastes

This term applies to manures produced by farm animals. It may also apply to arable wastes such as straw if these are disposed of other than by burning or composting on site. Waste pesticides and fertilizers are categorized as agricultural waste whilst they remain (or are disposed of) on the farm but, because of their chemical nature, are generally classified as special wastes if the farmer requires to dispose of them in a responsible manner off his land.

HAZARDOUS WASTES

General Definition

All wastes which have a harmful effect on the environment and on human health. This category includes special wastes but is also extended to other wastes not so defined. 'Hazardous' and 'difficult' are terms which have historically been applied to these wastes. However, the term 'hazardous' should now only apply to those wastes defined in the Directive on Hazardous Waste 1991 and controlled by the Transfrontier Shipment of Hazardous Waste Regulations 1988; the term 'difficult' has no legal meaning when applied to waste.

The various categories which are considered in this booklet are defined below and are limited to those for which a specific treatment or disposal route is required.

Special wastes

These are defined under the Control of Pollution Act 1974 as waste which 'is or may be so dangerous or difficult to dispose of that special provision... is required for (its) disposal'.

It is further defined as having a flashpoint of 21°C or less, of being capable of causing serious damage or death by ingestion ($5cm^3$ consumed by a child of 20kg) or of damage to skin tissue by exposure for 15 minutes or less.

PCBs

Polychlorinated biphenyls (PCBs) were originally added to transformer oils to improve electrical conductivity. They have since been found to persist and accumulate in the environment and to produce extremely toxic substances — dioxins and dibenzofurans — on partial combustion. A ban was placed on their sale or use in 1986. The waste may be in the form of liquids, solids or sludges.

Acid tars

Acid tars are produced from the acid washing of benzene, toluene and xylene fractions distilled from crude coal carbonization of benzol, from the production of lubricating oils and from refining waste oils. Principally a liquid waste, as produced, in some a sludge settles out on storage making handling difficult. They generally comprise 65–90 per cent sulphuric acid, up to 15 per cent organic compounds and up to 20 per cent water.

Metal-finishing wastes

These wastes are in the form of both liquids and sludges, and comprise acid pickle liquors and metal hydroxide sludges. They are inorganic.

Halogenated hydrocarbon solvents

These wastes may be in the form of a solid residue, a liquid oily waste or a sludge.

Cyanide wastes

Cyanide is toxic in certain forms, and less toxic in others. It was the discovery of indiscriminately-dumped cyanide wastes (see Chapter 6) that led to the Deposit of Poisonous Waste Act 1972. Cyanide wastes result from coal carbonization, metal plating and hardening, and are in the form of solid residues and liquors.

Clinical wastes

These are principally wastes from hospitals and nursing homes, and include bandages, dressings, syringes and various organic substances. They are not officially classed as hazardous wastes but require special handling and disposal, generally by incineration. They are specifically covered under the Collection and Disposal of Waste Regulations 1988.

RADIOACTIVE WASTES

Radioactive waste

Waste contaminated by reason of its radioactivity arising from a variety of sources including hospitals, nuclear power plants and defence installations. For disposal purposes, radioactive wastes are defined according to activity.

Low-level radioactive waste

Low-level wastes are quantitatively defined as wastes with an activity greater than very low level wastes (i.e. greater than 400 kBq $\beta+\gamma$ and less than 0.1 m³; or less than 40GBq $\beta +\gamma$ for single items) but less than 40Bq/tonne α and less than 12GBq /t $\beta+ \gamma$.

These wastes are usually materials such as used gloves and syringes.

Intermediate-level radioactive waste

Again, there is no precise definition, and activity ranges upwards from the upper limit of the low-level material. These wastes are generally 1000 times more active than low-level wastes.

High-level radioactive waste

Generally radioactive waste which generates heat is classed as high-level waste. These wastes normally only arise when spent nuclear fuel is dissolved in acid to separate the waste (fission products) from the re-usable uranium.

Bibliography and Some Further Sources of Information

Publications by the Department of the Environment, available from H.M. Stationery Office:

1. Waste Management Papers

Waste Management Paper No.	Date of Publication	Title
1	1976 Revision 1992	*Reclamation, Treatment and Disposal of Wastes – An Evaluation of Options*
2	1976	*Waste Disposal Surveys*
3	1976	*Guideline for the Preparation of a Waste Disposal Plan*
4	1st issued 1976 Re-issued 1988 Revised 1992	*The Licensing of Waste Disposal Sites*
5	1976	*The Relationship between Waste Disposal Authorities and Private Industry*
6	1976	*Polychlorinated Biphenyl (PCB) Wastes – A Technical Memorandum on Reclamation, Treatment and Disposal including a Code of Practice*
7	1976	*Mineral Oil Wastes – A Technical Memorandum on Arisings, Treatment and Disposal including a Code of Practice*
8	1976 Re-issued 1985	*Heat-Treatment Cyanide Wastes – A Technical Memorandum on Arisings, Treatment and Disposal including a Code of Practice*
9	1976	*Halogenated Hydrocarbon Solvent Wastes from Cleaning Processes – A Technical Memorandum on Reclamation and Disposal including a Code of Practice*
10	1976	*Local Authority Waste Disposal Statistics 1974–75*
11	1976	*Metal Finishing Wastes – A Technical Memorandum on Arisings, Treatment and Disposal including a Code of Practice.*

		Arisings, Treatment and Disposal including a Code of Practice
26	1986 Draft Revision November 1992	Landfilling Wastes – A Technical Memorandum for the Disposal of Wastes on Landfill Sites
27	1989 Re-issued 1991	The Control of Landfill Gas – A Technical Memorandum on the Monitoring and Control of Landfill Gas
28	1991	Recycling – A Memorandum for Local Authorities on Recycling

2. Reports of the Hazardous Waste Inspectorate

First Report	June 1985	Hazardous Waste Management: An Overview
Second Report	June 1986	Hazardous Waste Management: Ramshackle & Antediluvian
Third Report	June 1988	Hazardous Waste Inspectorate: Third Report

3. Reports of Her Majesty's Inspectorate of Pollution

First Report	March 1989	HMIP First Annual Report 1987–88
Second Report	August 1990	HMIP Second Annual Report 1988–89
Third Report	April 1991	HMIP Third Annual Report 1989–90
Fourth Report	October 1991	HMIP Fourth Annual Report 1990–91
Fifth Report	March 1993	HMIP Fifth Annual Report 1991–92
Sixth Report	October 1993	HMIP Sixth Annual Report 1992–93

4. Reports of the Royal Commission on Environmental Pollution

Eleventh Report	December 1985	Managing Waste: the Duty of Care. Cmnd. 9675
Twelfth Report	February 1988	Best Practicable Environmental Option. Cm. 310
Seventeenth Report	May 1993	Incineration of Waste. Cm. 2181

5. Government Committees

July 1981	House of Lords Select Committee on Science and Technology: Session 1980–81, First Report: Hazardous Waste Disposal
November 1984	Report of the Independent Review of Disposal of Radioactive Waste in the North East Atlantic

February 1989   House of Commons Session 1988–89 Environment
                 Committee Second Report: *Toxic Waste*

Other Useful Publications

Wilson, D.C.   *Waste Management: Planning, Evaluation, Technologies.*
                     1981. Oxford University Press
Holmes, J.E. (Ed)   *Practical Waste Management.* 1983. John Wiley & Sons
Porteous, A. (Ed)   *Hazardous Waste: Management Handbook.* 1985. Butterworths
Haigh, N.   *EEC Environmental Policy & Britain.* 2nd Edition 1987.
                     Longman Group UK Ltd
Coopers & Lybrand   *Landfill Costs and Prices: Correcting Possible Market
                     Distortions.* 1993. DoE
Department of the   *Digest of Environmental Protection and Water Statistics,*
  Environment   produced annually
Ibid   *Planning Policy Guidance Note 23,* DoE July 1994
National Rivers   Various documents, including a series of 17 (at the time of
  Authority   writing) on water quality Report No. 1: *Discharge consent and
                     compliance policy: a blueprint for the future* and Report No.
                     17: *Discharge consents and compliance: The NRA's approach
                     to control of discharges to water* are of particular relevance
Chartered Institution *An Introduction to Sewage Treatment*.* 1987
  of Water and
  Environmental
  Management
Ibid   *Sewage Sludge I: Production, Preliminary Treatment and
                     Digestion*.* 1979
Ibid   *Sewage Sludge II: Conditioning, Dewatering and Thermal
                     Drying*.* 1981
Ibid   *Sewage Sludge III: Utilization and Disposal*.* 1978

*Copies of these publications are obtainable from the Institution's Headquarters.

INDEX
Italic page numbers denote figures

INDEX

INDEX

INDEX

INDEX